CS-12   GENERAL APTITUDE AND ABILITIES SERIES

This is your
PASSBOOK for...

Clerical Abilities

Test Preparation Study Guide
Questions & Answers

COPYRIGHT NOTICE

This book is SOLELY intended for, is sold ONLY to, and its use is RESTRICTED to individual, bona fide applicants or candidates who qualify by virtue of having seriously filed applications for appropriate license, certificate, professional and/or promotional advancement, higher school matriculation, scholarship, or other legitimate requirements of education and/or governmental authorities.

This book is NOT intended for use, class instruction, tutoring, training, duplication, copying, reprinting, excerption, or adaptation, etc., by:

1) Other publishers
2) Proprietors and/or Instructors of "Coaching" and/or Preparatory Courses
3) Personnel and/or Training Divisions of commercial, industrial, and governmental organizations
4) Schools, colleges, or universities and/or their departments and staffs, including teachers and other personnel
5) Testing Agencies or Bureaus
6) Study groups which seek by the purchase of a single volume to copy and/or duplicate and/or adapt this material for use by the group as a whole without having purchased individual volumes for each of the members of the group
7) Et al.

Such persons would be in violation of appropriate Federal and State statutes.

PROVISION OF LICENSING AGREEMENTS – Recognized educational, commercial, industrial, and governmental institutions and organizations, and others legitimately engaged in educational pursuits, including training, testing, and measurement activities, may address request for a licensing agreement to the copyright owners, who will determine whether, and under what conditions, including fees and charges, the materials in this book may be used them. In other words, a licensing facility exists for the legitimate use of the material in this book on other than an individual basis. However, it is asseverated and affirmed here that the material in this book CANNOT be used without the receipt of the express permission of such a licensing agreement from the Publishers. Inquiries re licensing should be addressed to the company, attention rights and permissions department.

All rights reserved, including the right of reproduction in whole or in part, in any form or by any means, electronic or mechanical, including photocopying, recording, or by any information storage and retrieval system, without permission in writing from the Publisher.

Copyright © 2024 by
National Learning Corporation

212 Michael Drive, Syosset, NY 11791
(516) 921-8888 • www.passbooks.com
E-mail: info@passbooks.com

PASSBOOK® SERIES

THE *PASSBOOK® SERIES* has been created to prepare applicants and candidates for the ultimate academic battlefield – the examination room.

At some time in our lives, each and every one of us may be required to take an examination – for validation, matriculation, admission, qualification, registration, certification, or licensure.

Based on the assumption that every applicant or candidate has met the basic formal educational standards, has taken the required number of courses, and read the necessary texts, the *PASSBOOK® SERIES* furnishes the one special preparation which may assure passing with confidence, instead of failing with insecurity. Examination questions – together with answers – are furnished as the basic vehicle for study so that the mysteries of the examination and its compounding difficulties may be eliminated or diminished by a sure method.

This book is meant to help you pass your examination provided that you qualify and are serious in your objective.

The entire field is reviewed through the huge store of content information which is succinctly presented through a provocative and challenging approach – the question-and-answer method.

A climate of success is established by furnishing the correct answers at the end of each test.

You soon learn to recognize types of questions, forms of questions, and patterns of questioning. You may even begin to anticipate expected outcomes.

You perceive that many questions are repeated or adapted so that you can gain acute insights, which may enable you to score many sure points.

You learn how to confront new questions, or types of questions, and to attack them confidently and work out the correct answers.

You note objectives and emphases, and recognize pitfalls and dangers, so that you may make positive educational adjustments.

Moreover, you are kept fully informed in relation to new concepts, methods, practices, and directions in the field.

You discover that you are actually taking the examination all the time: you are preparing for the examination by "taking" an examination, not by reading extraneous and/or supererogatory textbooks.

In short, this PASSBOOK®, used directedly, should be an important factor in helping you to pass your test.

CLERICAL ABILITIES TESTS

This guide provides a general description of the subject areas to be tested and the different types of questions you will likely see on any of the tests in this series. The Examination Announcement will specify the exact subject areas to be included on the specific test you will be taking.

The Clerical Abilities Tests have an overall time allowance of 3 hours. They are divided into five subject areas and the questions are designed to evaluate the following abilities:

1. SPELLING: These questions test your ability to spell words that are used in written business communications.
2. ALPHABETIZING: These questions test your ability to file material in alphabetical order.
3. RECORD KEEPING: These questions evaluate your ability to perform common record keeping tasks. The test consists of two or more "sets" of questions; each set concerning a different problem. Typical record keeping problems might involve the organization or collation of data from several sources; scheduling; maintaining a record system using running balances; or completion of a table summarizing data using totals, subtotals, averages and percents.
4. CLERICAL OPERATIONS WITH LETTERS AND NUMBERS: These questions test your skills and abilities in clerical operations involving alphabetizing, comparing, checking and counting. The questions require you to follow the specific directions given for each question which may involve alphabetizing, comparing, checking and counting given groups of letters and/or numbers.
5. USING A DIRECTORY: These questions test your ability to keep directory records and to supply accurate information to callers. The questions require you to incorporate name and/or room changes into a current telephone directory and to answer questions, such as those that would be asked by callers, about the information contained in the directory listing.

The Examination Announcement will list two or more of the above subject areas to be included in the written test you will be taking. All written tests in the series include CLERICAL OPERATIONS WITH LETTERS AND NUMBERS.

The remainder of this guide explains how you are tested in each of these subject areas. A **TEST TASK** is provided for each subject. This is an explanation of how a question is presented and how to correctly answer it. Be sure to read each one carefully.

You will also be given at least one **SAMPLE QUESTION** for each subject area. It will be of the type that you will see on the actual test. The **SOLUTION** and correct answer are provided after each question. You should study the question and its solution until you understand how it works.

SUBJECT AREA 1

SPELLING: These questions test you ability to spell words that are used in written business communications.

TEST TASK: You are given questions that contain a list of words. You must determine which, if any, of the words is misspelled.

SAMPLE QUESTION:

Which one of the following words is misspelled?
A. manageable
B. circumstants
C. legality
D. None of the above is misspelled

The answer is B.

SOLUTION: *To answer this question, you must examine each of the words. The words "manageable" (choice A) and "legality" (choice C) are spelled correctly. The word "circumstants" (choice B) is misspelled. The correct spelling is "circumstance."*

SUBJECT AREA 2

ALPHABETIZING: These questions test your ability to file material in alphabetical order.

TEST TASK: You will be provided with a list of names. You must put the names into alphabetical order.

SAMPLE QUESTION:

Of the following, which one should be THIRD in an alphabetical file?
A. Docker, John
B. Decker, Jane
C. Dinckman, June
D. Dockman, James

The answer is A.

SOLUTION: *To answer this question, you must first put the names into alphabetical order. "Decker, Jane" would be first. "Dinckman, June" would be second. "Docker, John" would be third followed by "Dockman, James." The question asks for the third name on the list. The answer is "Docker, John" (choice A).*

SUBJECT AREA 3

RECORD KEEPING: These questions test your ability to perform common record keeping tasks.

TEST TASK: The questions in this subject area are contained in two or more sets. Each set presents a different problem. Typical record keeping problems might involve:
- organization or collation of data from several sources
- scheduling
- maintaining a record system using running balances
- completion of a table summarizing data using totals, subtotals, averages and percents

SAMPLE QUESTIONS:

The following two questions are based on the table below.

	NUMBER OF AUTOMOBILE ACCIDENTS BY LOCATION AND CAUSE (1998)			
	LOCATION 1		LOCATION 2	
CAUSE	Number	Percent	Number	Percent
Road Conditions	10	20	25	42
Drunk Drivers	20	40	5	8
Speeding	15	30	15	25
Unknown	5	10	15	25
TOTALS	50	100	60	100

QUESTION 1: Which of the following is the SECOND highest cause of accidents for both locations combined?
- A. Road Conditions
- B. Drunk Drivers
- C. Speeding
- D. Unknown

The answer is C

SOLUTION: *To answer this question, you must first add the number from location 1 to the number from location 2 for each accident cause. Then, you must rank the causes from highest to lowest based on the totals you obtain. You can then determine the second highest cause of accidents for both locations combined. In this example, "Road Conditions" (choice A) would be the highest cause of accidents with 35. The second highest cause of accidents is "Speeding" (choice C) with 30. The correct answer is "Speeding" (choice C).*

QUESTION 2: The average number of automobile accidents per week that occurred in Location 2 in 1998 (52 weeks) was most nearly
- A. 0.8
- B. 1.2
- C. 2.1
- D. 5.2

The answer is B

SOLUTION: *To answer this question, you must divide the total number of accidents in location 2 (60), by 52 weeks. The answer, rounded to the nearest tenth is 1.2 (choice B).*

SUBJECT AREA 4

CLERICAL OPERATIONS WITH LETTERS AND NUMBERS: These questions test your skills and abilities in clerical operations involving alphabetizing, comparing, checking and counting. The questions require you to follow the specific directions given for each question which may involve alphabetizing, comparing, checking and counting given groups of letters and/or numbers.

TEST TASK: You are given questions, which require you to follow specific directions given for each question. Each question may involve alphabetizing, comparing, checking and counting given groups of letters and/or numbers.

SAMPLE QUESTIONS:

QUESTION 1: How many pairs of the following groups of letters are exactly alike?

BRFQSX   BRFQSX
ACDOBJ   ACDBOJ
RPTQVS   RPTQVS
ZUYRVB   ZUYRVB
SPQRAS   SQRPAS
HVCBWR   HVCRWB

A. 2
B. 3
C. 4
D. 5

The answer is B.

SOLUTION: *To answer this question you must compare the column of letter groups on the left to the column of letter groups on the right. BRFQSX, RPTQVS and ZUYRVB of the left column are exactly like BRFQSX, RPTQVS and ZUYRVB of the right column. The other groups of letters are not exactly alike so the answer is 3 (choice B).*

QUESTION 2: In the following sentence, how many words contain letters that appear more than once in that word?

"Right around April Fool's Day, the daffodils and crocuses start to emerge and cheer us up after a long winter."

A. 5
B. 6
C. 7
D. 8

The answer is B.

SOLUTION: *To answer this question, look at each word to see how many contain the same letter at least twice. The words that do are: "Fool's," "daffodils," "crocuses," "start," "emerge," and "cheer." The total number of words is 6. The answer is 6 (choice B).*

SUBJECT AREA 4 (cont.)

QUESTION 3: Which one of the following letters is as far after C as T is after O in the alphabet?

  A. G
  B. H
  C. I
  D. J

The answer is B.

SOLUTION: *Count how many letters are between O and T in the alphabet. There are 4: P, Q, R and S. There are also 4 letters between C and H: D, E, F and G. The answer is H (choice B).*

QUESTION 4: In the following list of numbers, how many times does 8 come just after 6 when 6 comes just after an odd number?

    63256872534942368445768423 96868

  A. 2
  B. 3
  C. 4
  D. 5

The answer is C.

SOLUTION: *To answer this question, you must determine the number of times 8 follows 6 when 6 follows an odd number. There are 4 occasions where 8 follows 6 and the number 6 follows an odd number. They are 568, 368, 768 and 968. The answer is 4 (choice C).*

SUBJECT AREA 5

USING A DIRECTORY: These questions test your ability to keep directory records and to supply accurate information to callers.

TEST TASK: You will be provided with a telephone directory and a list of changes, and you will be asked to incorporate name and/or room changes into the directory. You will be asked to answer questions such as those that would be asked by callers about the information contained in the directory listing.

SAMPLE QUESTION:

Example: This question is based on the DIRECTORY and LIST OF CHANGES shown below:

DIRECTORY

NAME	RM. NO.	EXT.	NAME	RM. NO.	EXT.
Adams, Dave	123	1234	Charles, Bob	126	9109
Brown, Bill	125	5678	Davis, Ann	128	1112
Brull, Betty	142	5768	Diaz, Angel	134	2212
Calvin, Ed	155	2314	Evans, Sue	127	9502
Cerra, Lisa	116	4312	Frank, Chris	151	3456

LIST OF CHANGES in effect today:

All calls for persons not listed above should be referred to Ann Davis in Personnel.

Bill Brown is on vacation; his calls should be referred to Dave Adams whose extension has been changed to 8737.

QUESTION: To which one of the following extensions should a call for Marc Evans be directed?

A. 1112
B. 1234
C. 5678
D. 8737

Answer is A.

SOLUTION: *To answer this question, you must first determine that Marc Adams is not listed in the directory above, and that calls for people not so listed should be referred to Ann Davis in Personnel. Find Ann Davis in the directory; her extension is 1112 (choice A).*

CONCLUSION

You and your feelings about tests have a great deal to do with how you perform on a test. Some people get so tense and nervous that they don't do as well as they could. They forget things they know or make simple mistakes. The following suggestions should help you overcome these problems.

- Study and review this Guide to become familiar with the test contents.
- Give yourself plenty of time to do what you need to do before the test starts. Arrive at the test room a little ahead of the starting time.
- Try to relax just before the test starts.
- Listen carefully to the instructions the Monitors give you. Carefully read all instructions on the Candidate Directions you are given at the test as well as information on the covers of the test booklets.
- Try to keep calm, cool and collected throughout the test.
- Keep track of time.

HOW TO TAKE A TEST

You have studied long, hard and conscientiously.

With your official admission card in hand, and your heart pounding, you have been admitted to the examination room.

You note that there are several hundred other applicants in the examination room waiting to take the same test.

They all appear to be equally well prepared.

You know that nothing but your best effort will suffice. The "moment of truth" is at hand: you now have to demonstrate objectively, in writing, your knowledge of content and your understanding of subject matter.

You are fighting the most important battle of your life—to pass and/or score high on an examination which will determine your career and provide the economic basis for your livelihood.

What extra, special things should you know and should you do in taking the examination?

I. YOU MUST PASS AN EXAMINATION

A. WHAT EVERY CANDIDATE SHOULD KNOW
    Examination applicants often ask us for help in preparing for the written test. What can I study in advance? What kinds of questions will be asked? How will the test be given? How will the papers be graded?

B. HOW ARE EXAMS DEVELOPED?
    Examinations are carefully written by trained technicians who are specialists in the field known as "psychological measurement," in consultation with recognized authorities in the field of work that the test will cover. These experts recommend the subject matter areas or skills to be tested; only those knowledges or skills important to your success on the job are included. The most reliable books and source materials available are used as references. Together, the experts and technicians judge the difficulty level of the questions.
    Test technicians know how to phrase questions so that the problem is clearly stated. Their ethics do not permit "trick" or "catch" questions. Questions may have been tried out on sample groups, or subjected to statistical analysis, to determine their usefulness.
    Written tests are often used in combination with performance tests, ratings of training and experience, and oral interviews. All of these measures combine to form the best-known means of finding the right person for the right job.

II. HOW TO PASS THE WRITTEN TEST

A. BASIC STEPS

1) Study the announcement

How, then, can you know what subjects to study? Our best answer is: "Learn as much as possible about the class of positions for which you've applied." The exam will test the knowledge, skills and abilities needed to do the work.

Your most valuable source of information about the position you want is the official exam announcement. This announcement lists the training and experience qualifications. Check these standards and apply only if you come reasonably close to meeting them. Many jurisdictions preview the written test in the exam announcement by including a section called "Knowledge and Abilities Required," "Scope of the Examination," or some similar heading. Here you will find out specifically what fields will be tested.

2) Choose appropriate study materials

If the position for which you are applying is technical or advanced, you will read more advanced, specialized material. If you are already familiar with the basic principles of your field, elementary textbooks would waste your time. Concentrate on advanced textbooks and technical periodicals. Think through the concepts and review difficult problems in your field.

These are all general sources. You can get more ideas on your own initiative, following these leads. For example, training manuals and publications of the government agency which employs workers in your field can be useful, particularly for technical and professional positions. A letter or visit to the government department involved may result in more specific study suggestions, and certainly will provide you with a more definite idea of the exact nature of the position you are seeking.

3) Study this book!

III. KINDS OF TESTS

Tests are used for purposes other than measuring knowledge and ability to perform specified duties. For some positions, it is equally important to test ability to make adjustments to new situations or to profit from training. In others, basic mental abilities not dependent on information are essential. Questions which test these things may not appear as pertinent to the duties of the position as those which test for knowledge and information. Yet they are often highly important parts of a fair examination. For very general questions, it is almost impossible to help you direct your study efforts. What we can do is to point out some of the more common of these general abilities needed in public service positions and describe some typical questions.

1) General information

Broad, general information has been found useful for predicting job success in some kinds of work. This is tested in a variety of ways, from vocabulary lists to questions about current events. Basic background in some field of work, such as sociology or economics, may be sampled in a group of questions. Often these are principles which have become familiar to most persons through exposure rather than through formal training. It is difficult to advise you how to study for these questions; being alert to the world around you is our best suggestion.

2) Verbal ability

An example of an ability needed in many positions is verbal or language ability. Verbal ability is, in brief, the ability to use and understand words. Vocabulary and grammar tests are typical measures of this ability. Reading comprehension or paragraph interpretation questions are common in many kinds of civil service tests. You are given a paragraph of written material and asked to find its central meaning.

IV. KINDS OF QUESTIONS

1. Multiple-choice Questions

Most popular of the short-answer questions is the "multiple choice" or "best answer" question. It can be used, for example, to test for factual knowledge, ability to solve problems or judgment in meeting situations found at work.

A multiple-choice question is normally one of three types:
- It can begin with an incomplete statement followed by several possible endings. You are to find the one ending which best completes the statement, although some of the others may not be entirely wrong.
- It can also be a complete statement in the form of a question which is answered by choosing one of the statements listed.
- It can be in the form of a problem – again you select the best answer.

Here is an example of a multiple-choice question with a discussion which should give you some clues as to the method for choosing the right answer:

When an employee has a complaint about his assignment, the action which will best help him overcome his difficulty is to
- A. discuss his difficulty with his coworkers
- B. take the problem to the head of the organization
- C. take the problem to the person who gave him the assignment
- D. say nothing to anyone about his complaint

In answering this question, you should study each of the choices to find which is best. Consider choice "A" – Certainly an employee may discuss his complaint with fellow employees, but no change or improvement can result, and the complaint remains unresolved. Choice "B" is a poor choice since the head of the organization probably does not know what assignment you have been given, and taking your problem to him is known as "going over the head" of the supervisor. The supervisor, or person who made the assignment, is the person who can clarify it or correct any injustice. Choice "C" is, therefore, correct. To say nothing, as in choice "D," is unwise. Supervisors have and interest in knowing the problems employees are facing, and the employee is seeking a solution to his problem.

2. True/False

3. Matching Questions

Matching an answer from a column of choices within another column.

V. RECORDING YOUR ANSWERS

Computer terminals are used more and more today for many different kinds of exams.

For an examination with very few applicants, you may be told to record your answers in the test booklet itself. Separate answer sheets are much more common. If this separate answer sheet is to be scored by machine – and this is often the case – it is highly important that you mark your answers correctly in order to get credit.

VI. BEFORE THE TEST

YOUR PHYSICAL CONDITION IS IMPORTANT

If you are not well, you can't do your best work on tests. If you are half asleep, you can't do your best either. Here are some tips:

1) Get about the same amount of sleep you usually get. Don't stay up all night before the test, either partying or worrying—DON'T DO IT!
2) If you wear glasses, be sure to wear them when you go to take the test. This goes for hearing aids, too.
3) If you have any physical problems that may keep you from doing your best, be sure to tell the person giving the test. If you are sick or in poor health, you relay cannot do your best on any test. You can always come back and take the test some other time.

Common sense will help you find procedures to follow to get ready for an examination. Too many of us, however, overlook these sensible measures. Indeed, nervousness and fatigue have been found to be the most serious reasons why applicants fail to do their best on civil service tests. Here is a list of reminders:

- Begin your preparation early – Don't wait until the last minute to go scurrying around for books and materials or to find out what the position is all about.
- Prepare continuously – An hour a night for a week is better than an all-night cram session. This has been definitely established. What is more, a night a week for a month will return better dividends than crowding your study into a shorter period of time.
- Locate the place of the exam – You have been sent a notice telling you when and where to report for the examination. If the location is in a different town or otherwise unfamiliar to you, it would be well to inquire the best route and learn something about the building.
- Relax the night before the test – Allow your mind to rest. Do not study at all that night. Plan some mild recreation or diversion; then go to bed early and get a good night's sleep.
- Get up early enough to make a leisurely trip to the place for the test – This way unforeseen events, traffic snarls, unfamiliar buildings, etc. will not upset you.
- Dress comfortably – A written test is not a fashion show. You will be known by number and not by name, so wear something comfortable.
- Leave excess paraphernalia at home – Shopping bags and odd bundles will get in your way. You need bring only the items mentioned in the official notice you received; usually everything you need is provided. Do not bring reference books to the exam. They will only confuse those last minutes and be taken away from you when in the test room.

- Arrive somewhat ahead of time – If because of transportation schedules you must get there very early, bring a newspaper or magazine to take your mind off yourself while waiting.
- Locate the examination room – When you have found the proper room, you will be directed to the seat or part of the room where you will sit. Sometimes you are given a sheet of instructions to read while you are waiting. Do not fill out any forms until you are told to do so; just read them and be prepared.
- Relax and prepare to listen to the instructions
- If you have any physical problem that may keep you from doing your best, be sure to tell the test administrator. If you are sick or in poor health, you really cannot do your best on the exam. You can come back and take the test some other time.

VII. AT THE TEST

The day of the test is here and you have the test booklet in your hand. The temptation to get going is very strong. Caution! There is more to success than knowing the right answers. You must know how to identify your papers and understand variations in the type of short-answer question used in this particular examination. Follow these suggestions for maximum results from your efforts:

1) Cooperate with the monitor

The test administrator has a duty to create a situation in which you can be as much at ease as possible. He will give instructions, tell you when to begin, check to see that you are marking your answer sheet correctly, and so on. He is not there to guard you, although he will see that your competitors do not take unfair advantage. He wants to help you do your best.

2) Listen to all instructions

Don't jump the gun! Wait until you understand all directions. In most civil service tests you get more time than you need to answer the questions. So don't be in a hurry. Read each word of Instructions until you clearly understand the meaning. Study the examples, listen to all announcements and follow directions. Ask questions if you do not understand what to do.

3) Identify your papers

Civil service exams are usually identified by number only. You will be assigned a number; you must not put your name on your test papers. Be sure to copy your number correctly. Since more than one exam may be given, copy your exact examination title.

4) Plan your time

Unless you are told that a test is a "speed" or "rate of work" test, speed itself is usually not important. Time enough to answer all the questions will be provided, but this does not mean that you have all day. An overall time limit has been set. Divide the total time (in minutes) by the number of questions to determine the approximate time you have for each question.

5) Do not linger over difficult questions

If you come across a difficult question, mark it with a paper clip (useful to have along) and come back to it when you have been through the booklet. One caution if you do this – be sure to skip a number on your answer sheet as well. Check often to be sure that you have not lost your place and that you are marking in the row numbered the same as the question you are answering.

6) Read the questions

Be sure you know what the question asks! Many capable people are unsuccessful because they failed to read the questions correctly.

7) Answer all questions

Unless you have been instructed that a penalty will be deducted for incorrect answers, it is better to guess than to omit a question.

8) Speed tests

It is often better NOT to guess on speed tests. It has been found that on timed tests people are tempted to spend the last few seconds before time is called in marking answers at random – without even reading them – in the hope of picking up a few extra points. To discourage this practice, the instructions may warn you that your score will be "corrected" for guessing. That is, a penalty will be applied. The incorrect answers will be deducted from the correct ones, or some other penalty formula will be used.

9) Review your answers

If you finish before time is called, go back to the questions you guessed or omitted to give them further thought. Review other answers if you have time.

10) Return your test materials

If you are ready to leave before others have finished or time is called, take ALL your materials to the monitor and leave quietly. Never take any test material with you. The monitor can discover whose papers are not complete, and taking a test booklet may be grounds for disqualification.

VIII. EXAMINATION TECHNIQUES

1) Read the general instructions carefully. These are usually printed on the first page of the exam booklet. As a rule, these instructions refer to the timing of the examination; the fact that you should not start work until the signal and must stop work at a signal, etc. If there are any special instructions, such as a choice of questions to be answered, make sure that you note this instruction carefully.

2) When you are ready to start work on the examination, that is as soon as the signal has been given, read the instructions to each question booklet, underline any key words or phrases, such as least, best, outline, describe and the like. In this way you will tend to answer as requested rather than discover on reviewing your paper that you listed without describing, that you selected the worst choice rather than the best choice, etc.

3) If the examination is of the objective or multiple-choice type – that is, each question will also give a series of possible answers: A, B, C or D, and you are called upon to select the best answer and write the letter next to that answer on your answer paper – it is advisable to start answering each question in turn. There may be anywhere from 50 to 100 such questions in the three or four hours allotted and you can see how much time would be taken if you read through all the questions before beginning to answer any. Furthermore, if you

come across a question or group of questions which you know would be difficult to answer, it would undoubtedly affect your handling of all the other questions.

4) If the examination is of the essay type and contains but a few questions, it is a moot point as to whether you should read all the questions before starting to answer any one. Of course, if you are given a choice – say five out of seven and the like – then it is essential to read all the questions so you can eliminate the two that are most difficult. If, however, you are asked to answer all the questions, there may be danger in trying to answer the easiest one first because you may find that you will spend too much time on it. The best technique is to answer the first question, then proceed to the second, etc.

5) Time your answers. Before the exam begins, write down the time it started, then add the time allowed for the examination and write down the time it must be completed, then divide the time available somewhat as follows:
   - If 3-1/2 hours are allowed, that would be 210 minutes. If you have 80 objective-type questions, that would be an average of 2-1/2 minutes per question. Allow yourself no more than 2 minutes per question, or a total of 160 minutes, which will permit about 50 minutes to review.
   - If for the time allotment of 210 minutes there are 7 essay questions to answer, that would average about 30 minutes a question. Give yourself only 25 minutes per question so that you have about 35 minutes to review.

6) The most important instruction is to read each question and make sure you know what is wanted. The second most important instruction is to time yourself properly so that you answer every question. The third most important instruction is to answer every question. Guess if you have to but include something for each question. Remember that you will receive no credit for a blank and will probably receive some credit if you write something in answer to an essay question. If you guess a letter – say "B" for a multiple-choice question – you may have guessed right. If you leave a blank as an answer to a multiple-choice question, the examiners may respect your feelings but it will not add a point to your score. Some exams may penalize you for wrong answers, so in such cases only, you may not want to guess unless you have some basis for your answer.

7) Suggestions
   a. Objective-type questions
      1. Examine the question booklet for proper sequence of pages and questions
      2. Read all instructions carefully
      3. Skip any question which seems too difficult; return to it after all other questions have been answered
      4. Apportion your time properly; do not spend too much time on any single question or group of questions
      5. Note and underline key words – all, most, fewest, least, best, worst, same, opposite, etc.
      6. Pay particular attention to negatives
      7. Note unusual option, e.g., unduly long, short, complex, different or similar in content to the body of the question
      8. Observe the use of "hedging" words – probably, may, most likely, etc.

9. Make sure that your answer is put next to the same number as the question
10. Do not second-guess unless you have good reason to believe the second answer is definitely more correct
11. Cross out original answer if you decide another answer is more accurate; do not erase until you are ready to hand your paper in
12. Answer all questions; guess unless instructed otherwise
13. Leave time for review

b. Essay questions
 1. Read each question carefully
 2. Determine exactly what is wanted. Underline key words or phrases.
 3. Decide on outline or paragraph answer
 4. Include many different points and elements unless asked to develop any one or two points or elements
 5. Show impartiality by giving pros and cons unless directed to select one side only
 6. Make and write down any assumptions you find necessary to answer the questions
 7. Watch your English, grammar, punctuation and choice of words
 8. Time your answers; don't crowd material

8) Answering the essay question

Most essay questions can be answered by framing the specific response around several key words or ideas. Here are a few such key words or ideas:

M's: manpower, materials, methods, money, management
P's: purpose, program, policy, plan, procedure, practice, problems, pitfalls, personnel, public relations

a. Six basic steps in handling problems:
 1. Preliminary plan and background development
 2. Collect information, data and facts
 3. Analyze and interpret information, data and facts
 4. Analyze and develop solutions as well as make recommendations
 5. Prepare report and sell recommendations
 6. Install recommendations and follow up effectiveness

b. Pitfalls to avoid
 1. Taking things for granted – A statement of the situation does not necessarily imply that each of the elements is necessarily true; for example, a complaint may be invalid and biased so that all that can be taken for granted is that a complaint has been registered
 2. Considering only one side of a situation – Wherever possible, indicate several alternatives and then point out the reasons you selected the best one
 3. Failing to indicate follow up – Whenever your answer indicates action on your part, make certain that you will take proper follow-up action to see how successful your recommendations, procedures or actions turn out to be
 4. Taking too long in answering any single question – Remember to time your answers properly

EXAMINATION SECTION

CLERICAL ABILITIES TEST

Clerical aptitude involves the ability to perceive pertinent detail in verbal or tabular material, to observe differences in copy, to proofread words and numbers, and to avoid perceptual errors in arithmetic computation.

NATURE OF THE TEST

Four types of clerical aptitude questions are presented in the Clerical Abilities Test. There are 120 questions with a short time limit. The test contains 30 questions on name and number checking, 30 on the arrangement of names in correct alphabetical order, 30 on simple arithmetic, and 30 on inspecting groups of letters and numbers. The questions have been arranged in groups or cycles of five questions of each type. The Clerical Abilities Test is primarily a test of speed in carrying out relatively simple clerical tasks. While accuracy on these tasks is important and will be taken into account in the scoring, experience has shown that many persons are so concerned about accuracy that they do the test more slowly than they should. Competitors should be cautioned that speed as well as accuracy is important to achieve a good score.

HOW THE TEST IS ADMINISTERED

Each competitor should be given a copy of the test booklet with sample questions on the cover page, an answer sheet, and a medium No. 2 pencil. Ten minutes are allowed to study the directions and sample questions and to answer the questions in the proper boxes on the two pages.
The separate answer sheet should be used for the test proper. Fifteen minutes are allowed for the test.

HOW THE TEST IS SCORED

The correct answers should be counted and recorded. The number of incorrect answers must also be counted because one-fourth of the number of incorrect answers is subtracted from the number of right answers. An omission is considered as neither a right nor a wrong answer. The score on this test is the number of right answers minus one-fourth of the number of wrong answers (fractions of one-half or less are dropped). For example, if an applicant had answered 89 questions correctly and 10 questions incorrectly, and had omitted 1 question, his score would be 87.

EXAMINATION SECTION

DIRECTIONS: This test contains four kinds of questions. There are some of each kind on each page in the booklet. The time limit for the test will be announced by the examiner.
Use the special pencil furnished by the examiner in marking your answers on the separate answer sheet. For each question, there are five suggested answers. Decide which answer is correct, find the number of the question on the answer sheet, and make a solid black mark between the dotted lines just below the letter of your answer. If you wish to change your answer, erase the first mark completely, do not merely cross it out.

SAMPLE QUESTIONS

In each line across the page there are three names or numbers that are much alike. Compare the three names or numbers and decide which ones are exactly alike. On the Sample Answer Sheet at the right, mark the answer
- A. if ALL THREE names or numbers are exactly ALIKE
- B. if only the FIRST and SECOND names or numbers are exactly ALIKE
- C. if only the FIRST and THIRD names or numbers are exactly ALIKE
- D. if only the SECOND and THIRD names or numbers are exactly ALIKE
- E. if ALL THREE names or numbers are DIFFERENT

I.	Davis Hazen	David Hozen	David Hazen
II.	Lois Appel	Lois Appel	Lois Apfel
III.	June Allan	Jane Allan	Jane Allan
IV.	10235	10235	10235
V.	32614	32164	32614

It will be to your advantage to learn what A, B, C, D, and E stand for. If you finish the sample questions before you are told to turn to the test, study them.

In the next group of sample questions, there is a name in a box at the left, and four other names in alphabetical order at the right. Find the correct space for the boxed name so that it will be in alphabetical order with the others, and mark the letter of that space as your answer.

VI. [Jones, Jane]

A. →
  Goodyear, G.L.
B. →
  Haddon, Harry
C. →
  Jackson, Mary
D. →
  Jenkins, William
E. →

VII. [Kessler, Neilson]

A. →
  Kessel, Carl
B. →
  Kessinger, D.J.
C. →
  Kessler, Karl
D. →
  Kessner, Lewis
E. →

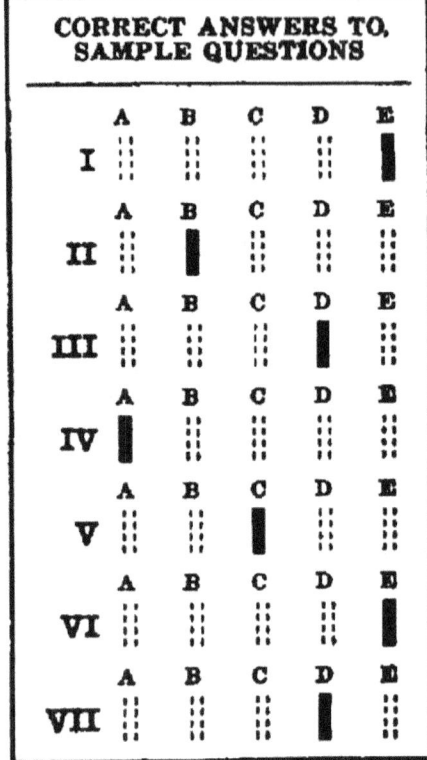

DIRECTIONS: In the following questions, complete the equation and find your answer among the list of suggested answers. Mark the Sample Answer Sheet A, B, C, or D for the answer you obtained; or if your answer is not among these, mark E for that question.

VIII. Add: 22
           +33

A. 44   B. 45   C. 54   D. 55   E. None of these

IX. Subtract: 24
              - 3

A. 20   B. 21   C. 27   D. 29   E. None of these

X. Multiply: 25
             x 5

A. 100   B. 115   C. 125   D. 135   E. None of these

XI. Divide: 6/126̄

    A. 20   B. 22   C. 24   D. 26   E. None of these

DIRECTIONS: There is one set of suggested answers for the next group of sample questions. Do not try to memorize these answers, because there will be a different set on each age in the test.

To find the answer to a question, find which suggested answer contains numbers and letters, all of which appear in the question. If no suggested answer fits, mark E for that question.

XII. 8 N K 9 G T 4 6

XIII. T 9 7 Z 6 L 3 K

XIV. Z 7 G K 3 9 8 N

XV. 3 K 9 4 6 G Z L

XVI. Z N 7 3 8 K T 9

Suggested Answers
A = 7, 9, G, K
B = 8, 9, T, Z
C = 6, 7, K, Z
D = 6, 8, G, T
E = None of the above

After you have marked your answers to all the questions on the Sample Answer Sheets on this page and on the front page of the booklet, check them with the answers in the boxes marked Correct Answers To Sample Questions.

Questions 1-5.

In Questions 1 through 5, compare the three names or numbers, and mark
    A. if ALL THREE names or numbers are exactly ALIKE
    B. if only the FIRST and SECOND names or numbers are exactly ALIKE
    C. if only the FIRST and THIRD names or numbers are exactly ALIKE
    D. if only the SECOND and THIRD names or numbers are exactly ALIKE
    E. if ALL THREE names or numbers are DIFFERENT

1.	5261383	5261383	5261338
2.	8125690	8126690	8125609
3.	W.E. Johnston	W.E. Johnson	W.E. Johnson
4.	Vergil L. Muller	Vergil L. Muller	Vergil L. Muller

5. Atherton R. Warde   Asheton R. Warde   Atherton P. Warde

Questions 6-10.

In Questions 6 through 10, find the correct place for the name in the box

6. | Hackett, Gerald |

A. →
   Habert, James
B. →
   Hachett, J.J.
C. →
   Hachetts, K. Larson
D. →
   Hachettson, Leroy
E. →

7. | Margenroth, Alvin |

A. →
   Margeroth, Albert
B. →
   Margestein, Dan
C. →
   Margestein, David
D. →
   Margue, Edgar
E. →

8. | Bobbitt, Olivier E. |

A. →
   Bobbitt, D. Olivier
B. →
   Bobbitt, Olivia B
C. →
   Bobbitt, Olivia H.
D. →
   Bobbitt, R. Olivia
E. →

9. | Mosley, Werner |

A. →
   Mosely, Albert J.
B. →
   Mosley, Alvin
C. →
   Mosley, S.M.
D. →
   Mozley, Vinson N.
E. →

10. | Youmuns, Frank L. |

   A. →
      Youmons, Frank G.
   B. →
      Youmons, Frank H.
   C. →
      Youmons, Frank K.
   D. →
      Youmons, Frank M.
   E. →

Questions 11-15.

11. Add: 43
         +32

    A. 55   B. 65   C. 66   D. 75   E. None of these

12. Subtract: 83
              - 4

    A. 73   B. 79   C. 80   D. 89   E. None of these

13. Multiply: 41
              x 7

    A. 281   B. 287   C. 291   D. 297   E. None of these

14. Divide: 6/306

    A. 44   B. 51   C. 52   D. 60   E. None of these

15. Add: 37
         +15

    A. 42   B. 52   C. 53   D. 62   E. None of these

Questions 16-20.

In Questions 16 through 20, find which one of the suggested answers appears in that question.

16. 6 2 5 K 4 P T G

17. L 4 7 2 T 6 V K

18. 3 5 4 L 9 V T G

19. G 4 K 7 L 3 5 Z

SUGGESTED ANSWERS
A = 4, 5, K, T
B = 4, 7, G, K
C = 2, 5, G, L
D = 2, 7, L, T
E = None of the above

20. 4 K 2 9 N 5 T G

Questions 21-25.

In Questions 21 through 25, compare the three names or numbers, and mark
- A. if ALL THREE names or numbers are exactly ALIKE
- B. if only the FIRST and SECOND names or numbers are exactly ALIKE
- C. if only the FIRST and THIRD names or numbers are exactly ALIKE
- D. if only the SECOND and THIRD names or numbers are exactly ALIKE
- E. if ALL THREE names or numbers are DIFFERENT

21.	2395890	2395890	2395890
22.	1926341	1926347	1926314
23.	E. Owens McVey	E. Owen McVey	E. Owen McVay
24.	Emily Neal Rouse	Emily Neal Rowse	Emily Neal Rowse
25.	H. Merritt Audubon	H. Merriott Audubon	H. Merritt Audubon

Questions 26-30.

In Questions 26 through 30, find the correct place for the name in the box.

26. Watters, N.O.
- A. →
  Waters, Charles L.
- B. →
  Waterson, Nina P.
- C. →
  Watson, Nora J.
- D. →
  Wattwood, Paul A.
- E. →

27. Johnston, Edward
- A. →
  Johnston, Edgar R.
- B. →
  Johnston, Edmond
- C. →
  Johnston, Edmund
- D. →
  Johnstone, Edmund A.
- E. →

28. | Rensch, Adeline | A. →
    Ramsay, Amos
    B. →
    Remschel, Augusta
    C. →
    Renshaw, Austin
    D. →
    Rentzel, Becky
    E. →

29. | Schnyder, Maurice | A. →
    Schneider, Martin
    B. →
    Schneider, Mertens
    C. →
    Schnyder, Newman
    D. →
    Schreibner, Norman
    E. →

30. | Freedenburg, C. Erma | A. →
    Freedenberg, Emerson
    B. →
    Freedenberg, Erma
    C. →
    Freedenberg, Erma E.
    D. →
    Freedinberg, Erma F.
    E. →

Questions 31-35.

31. Subtract: 68
              - 47

    A. 10   B. 11   C. 20   D. 22   E. None of these

32. Multiply: 50
               x 8

    A. 400   B. 408   C. 450   D. 458   E. None of these

33. Divide: 9/180

    A. 20   B. 29   C. 30   D. 39   E. None of these

34. Add: 78
          + 63

    A. 131   B. 140   C. 141   D. 151   E. None of these

35. Add: 89
     -70

    A. 9 B. 18 C. 19 D. 29 E. None of these

Questions 36-40.

In Questions 36 through 40, find which one of the suggested answers appears in that question.

36. 9 G Z 3 L 4 6 N

37. L 5 N K 4 3 9 V

38. 8 2 V P 9 L Z 5

39. V P 9 Z 5 L 8 7

40. 5 T 8 N 2 9 V L

SUGGESTED ANSWERS
A = 4, 9, L, V
B = 4, 5, N, Z
C = 5, 8, L, Z
D = 8, 9, N, V
E = None of the above

Questions 41-45.

In Questions 41 through 45, compare the three names or numbers, and mark
    A. if ALL THREE names or numbers are exactly ALIKE
    B. if only the FIRST and SECOND names or numbers are exactly ALIKE
    C. if only the FIRST and THIRD names or numbers are exactly ALIKE
    D. if only the SECOND and THIRD names or numbers are exactly ALIKE
    E. if ALL THREE names or numbers are DIFFERENT

41.	6219354	621354	6219354
42.	2312793	2312793	2312793
43.	1065407	1065407	1065047
44.	Francis Ransdell	Frances Ramsdell	Francis Ramsdell
45.	Cornelius Detwiler	Cornelius Detwiler	Cornelius Detwiler

Questions 46-50.

In Questions 46 through 50, find the correct place for the name in the box.

46. | DeMattia, Jessica |

A. →
  DeLong, Jesse
B. →
  DeMatteo, Jessie
C. →
  Derby, Jessie S.
D. →
  DeShazo, L.M.
E. →

47. | Theriault, Louis |

A. →
  Therien, Annette
B. →
  Therien, Elaine
C. →
  Thibeault, Gerald
D. →
  Thiebeault, Pierre
E. →

48. | Gaston, M. Hubert |

A. →
  Gaston, Dorothy M.
B. →
  Gaston, Henry N.
C. →
  Gaston, Isabel
D. →
  Gaston, M. Melvin
E. →

49. | SanMiguel, Carlos |

A. →
  SanLuis, Juana
B. →
  Santilli, Laura
C. →
  Stinnett, Nellie
D. →
  Stoddard, Victor
E. →

50. | DeLaTour, Hall F. |

A. →
   DeLargy, Harold
B. →
   DeLathouder, Hilda
C. →
   Lathrop, Hillary
D. →
   LaTour, Hulbert E.
E. →

Questions 51-55.

51. Multiply: 62
             x 5

    A. 300   B. 310   C. 315   D. 360   E. None of these

52. Divide: 3/153

    A. 41   B. 43   C. 51   D. 53   E. None of these

53. Add: 47
        +21

    A. 58   B. 59   C. 67   D. 68   E. None of these

54. Subtract: 87
             - 42

    A. 34   B. 35   C. 44   D. 45   E. None of these

55. Multiply: 37
             x 3

    A. 91   B. 101   C. 104   D. 114   E. None of these

Questions 56-60.

For Questions 56 through 60, find which one of the suggested answers appears in that question.

56. N 5 4 7 T K 3 Z

57. 8 5 3 V L 2 Z N

58. 7 2 5 N 9 K L V

59. 9 8 L 2 5 Z K V

60. Z 6 5 V 9 3 P N

SUGGESTED ANSWERS
A = 3, 8, K, N
B = 5, 8, N, V
C = 3, 9, V, Z
D = 5, 9, K, Z
E = None of the above

Questions 61-65.

In Questions 61 through 65, compare the three names or numbers, and mark
  A. if ALL THREE names or numbers are exactly ALIKE
  B. if only the FIRST and SECOND names or numbers are exactly ALIKE
  C. if only the FIRST and THIRD names or numbers are exactly ALIKE
  D. if only the SECOND and THIRD names or numbers are exactly ALIKE
  E. if ALL THREE names or numbers are DIFFERENT

61.	6452054	6452654	6452054
62.	8501268	8501268	8501286
63	Ella Burk Newham	Ella Burk Newnham	Elena Burk Newnham
64.	Jno. K. Ravencroft	Jno. H. Ravencroft	Jno. H. Ravencoft
65.	Martin Wills Pullen	Martin Wills Pulen	Martin Wills Pullen

Questions 66-70.

In Questions 66 through 70, find the correct place for the name in the box.

66. | O'Bannon, M.J. |

A. →
    O'Beirne, B.B.
B. →
    Oberlin, E.L.
C. →
    Oberneir, L.P.
D. →
    O'Brian, S.F.
E. →

67. | Entsminger, Jacob |

A. →
    Ensminger, J.
B. →
    Entsminger, J.A.
C. →
    Entsminger, Jack
D. →
    Entsminger, James
E. →

68. Iacone, Pete R.

A. →
   Iacone, Pedro
B. →
   Iacone, Pedro M.
C. →
   Iacone, Peter F.
D. →
   Iascone, Peter W.
E. →

69. Sheppard, Gladys

A. →
   Shepard, Dwight
B. →
   Shepard, F.H.
C. →
   Shephard, Louise
D. →
   Shepperd, Stella
E. →

70. Thackton, Melvin T.

A. →
   Thackston, Milton G.
B. →
   Thackston, Milton W.
C. →
   Thackston, Theodore
D. →
   Thackston, Thomas G.
E. →

Questions 71-75.

71. Divide: 7/357

   A. 51   B. 52   C. 53   D. 54   E. None of these

72. Add: 58
         +27

   A. 75   B. 84   C. 85   D. 95   E. None of these

73. Subtract: 86
              - 57

   A. 18   B. 29   C. 38   D. 39   E. None of these

74. Multiply: 68
              x 4

   A. 242   B. 264   C. 272   D. 274   E. None of these

75. Divide: 9/639̄

   A. 71   B. 73   C. 81   D. 83   E. None of these

Questions 76-80.

For Questions 76 through 80, find which one of the suggested answers appears in that question.

76. 6 Z T N 8 7 4 V   SUGGESTED ANSWERS
                              A = 2, 7, L, N
77. V 7 8 6 N 5 P L   B = 2, 8, T, V
                              C = 6, 8, L, T
78. N 7 P V 8 4 2 L   D = 6, 7, N, V
                              E = None of the above
79. 7 8 G 4 3 V L T

80. 4 8 G 2 T N 6 L

Questions 81-85.

In Questions 81 through 85, compare the three names or numbers, and mark
   A. if ALL THREE names or numbers are exactly ALIKE
   B. if only the FIRST and SECOND names or numbers are exactly ALIKE
   C. if only the FIRST and THIRD names or numbers are exactly ALIKE
   D. if only the SECOND and THIRD names or numbers are exactly ALIKE
   E. if ALL THREE names or numbers are DIFFERENT

81. 3457988   3457986   3457986

82. 4695682   4695862   4695682

83. Stricklund Kanedy Stricklund Kanedy Stricklund Kanedy

84. Joy Harbor Witner Joy Harloe Witner Joy Harloe Witner

85. R.M.O. Uberroth   R.M.O. Uberroth   R.N.O. Uberroth

Questions 86-90.

In Questions 86 through 90, find the correct place for the name in the box.

86. Dunlavey, M. Hilary

A. →
Dunleavy, Hilary G.
B. →
Dunleavy, Hilary K.
C. →
Dunleavy, Hilary S.
D. →
Dunleavy, Hilery W.
E. →

87. Yarbrough, Maria

A. →
Yabroudy, Margy
B. →
Yarboro, Marie
C. →
Yarborough, Marina
D. →
Yarborough, Mary
E. →

88. Prouty, Martha

A. →
Proutey, Margaret
B. →
Proutey, Maude
C. →
Prouty, Myra
D. →
Prouty, Naomi
E. →

89. Pawlowicz, Ruth M.

A. →
Pawalek, Edward
B. →
Pawelek, Flora G.
C. →
Pawlowski, Joan M.
D. →
Pawtowski, Wanda
E. →

90. | Vanstory, George |

A. →
   Vanover, Eva
B. →
   VanSwinderen, Floyd
C. →
   VanSyckle, Harry
D. →
   Vanture, Laurence
E. →

Questions 91-95

91. Add: 28
         +35

   A. 53   B. 62   C. 64   D. 73   E. None of these

92. Subtract: 78
              -69

   A. 7   B. 8   C. 18   D. 19   E. None of these

93. Multiply: 86
              x 6

   A. 492   B. 506   C. 516   D. 526   E. None of these

94. Divide: 8/648

   A. 71   B. 76   C. 81   D. 89   E. None of these

95. Add: 97
         +34

   A. 131   B. 132   C. 140   D. 141   E. None of these

Questions 96-100.

For Questions 96 through 100, find which one of the suggested answers appears in that question.

96. V 5 7 Z N 9 4 T

97. 4 6 P T 2 N K 9

98. 6 4 N 2 P 8 Z K

99. 7 P 5 2 4 N K T

100. K T 8 5 4 N 2 P

SUGGESTED ANSWERS
A = 2, 5, N, Z
B = 4, 5, N, P
C = 2, 9, P, T
D = 4, 9, T, Z
E = None of the above

Questions 101-105.

In Questions 101 through 105, compare the three names or numbers, and mark
- A. if ALL THREE names or numbers are exactly ALIKE
- B. if only the FIRST and SECOND names or numbers are exactly ALIKE
- C. if only the FIRST and THIRD names or numbers are exactly ALIKE
- D. if only the SECOND and THIRD names or numbers are exactly ALIKE
- E. if ALL THREE names or numbers are DIFFERENT

101.	1592514	1592574	1592574
102.	2010202	2010202	2010220
103.	6177396	6177936	6177396
104.	Drusilla S. Ridgeley	Drusilla S. Ridgeley	Drusilla S. Ridgeley
105.	Andrei I. Toumantzev	Andrei I. Tourmantzev	Andrei I. Toumantzov

Questions 106-110.

In Questions 106 through 110, find the correct place for the name in the box.

106. Fitzsimmons, Hugh

A. →
Fitts, Harold
B. →
Fitzgerald, June
C. →
FitzGibbon, Junius
D. →
FitzSimons, Martin
E. →

107. D'Amato, Vincent

A. →
Daly, Steven
B. →
D'Amboise, S. Vincent
C. →
Daniel, Vail
D. →
DeAlba, Valentina
E. →

108. | Schaeffer, Roger D. |

A. →
   Schaffert, Evelyn M.
B. →
   Schaffner, Margaret M.
C. →
   Schafhirt, Milton G.
D. →
   Shafer, Richard E.
E. →

109. | White-Lewis, Cecil |

A. →
   Whitelaw, Cordelia
B. →
   White-Leigh, Nancy
C. →
   Whitely, Rodney
D. →
   Whitlock, Warren
E. →

110. | VanDerHeggen, Don |

A. →
   VanDemark, Doris
B. →
   Vandenberg, H.E.
C. →
   VanDercook, Marie
D. →
   vanderLinden, Robert
E. →

Questions 111-115.

111. Add: 75
         +49

   A. 124   B. 125   C. 134   D. 225   E. None of these

112. Subtract: 69
              - 45

   A. 14   B. 23   C. 24   D. 26   E. None of these

113. Multiply: 36
               x 8

   A. 246   B. 262   C. 288   D. 368   E. None of these

114. Divide: 8/$\overline{328}$

   A. 31   B. 41   C. 42   D. 48   E. None of these

115. Multiply: 58
              x 9

   A. 472   B. 513   C. 521   D. 522   E. None of these

Questions 116-120.

For Questions 116 through 120, find which one of the suggested answers appears in that question.

116. Z 3 N P G 5 4 2

117. 6 N 2 8 G 4 P T

118. 6 N 4 T V G 8 2

119. T 3 P 4 N 8 G 2

120. 6 7 K G N 2 L 5

SUGGESTED ANSWERS:
A = 2, 3, G, N
B = 2, 6, N, T
C = 3, 4, G, K
D = 4, 6, K, T
E = None of the above

KEY (CORRECT ANSWERS)

1.	B	21.	A	41.	A	61.	C	81.	D	101.	D
2.	E	22.	E	42.	A	62.	B	82.	C	102.	B
3.	D	23.	E	43.	B	63.	E	83.	A	103.	C
4.	A	24.	D	44.	E	64.	E	84.	D	104.	A
5.	E	25.	C	45.	A	65.	C	85.	B	105.	E
6.	E	26.	D	46.	C	66.	A	86.	A	106.	D
7.	A	27.	D	47.	A	667.	D	87.	E	107.	B
8.	D	28.	C	48.	D	68.	C	88.	C	108.	A
9.	B	29.	C	49.	B	69.	D	89.	C	109.	C
10.	E	30.	D	50.	C	70.	E	90.	B	110.	D
11.	D	31.	E	51.	B	71.	A	91.	E	111.	A
12.	B	32.	A	52.	C	72.	C	92.	E	112.	C
13.	B	33.	A	53.	D	73.	B	93.	C	113.	C
14.	B	34.	C	54.	D	74.	C	94.	C	114.	B
15.	B	35.	C	55.	E	75.	A	95.	A	115.	D
16.	A	36.	E	56.	E	76.	D	96.	D	116.	A
17.	D	37.	A	57.	B	77.	D	97.	C	117.	B
18.	E	38.	C	58.	E	78.	A	98.	E	118.	B
19.	B	39.	C	59.	D	79.	E	99.	B	119.	A
20.	A	40.	D	60.	C	80.	C	100.	B	120.	E

CLERICAL ABILITIES TEST
EXAMINATION SECTION
TEST 1

DIRECTIONS: Each question or incomplete statement is followed by several suggested answers or completions. Select the one that BEST answers the question or completes the statement. *PRINT THE LETTER OF THE CORRECT ANSWER IN THE SPACE AT THE RIGHT.*

Questions 1-10.

DIRECTIONS: Questions 1 through 10 consist of lines of names, dates, and numbers. For each question, you are to choose the option (A, B, C, or D) in Column II which EXACTLY matches the information in Column I. *PRINT THE LETTER OF THE CORRECT ANSWER IN THE SPACE AT THE RIGHT.*

SAMPLE QUESTION

Column I
Schneider 11/16/75 581932

Column II
A. Schneider 11/16/75 518932
B. Schneider 11/16/75 581932
C. Schnieder 11/16/75 581932
D. Shnieder 11/16/75 518932

The correct answer is B. Only Option B shows the name, date, and number exactly as they are in Column I. Option A has a mistake in the number. Option C has a mistake in the name. Option D has a mistake in the name and in the number. Now answer Questions 1 through 10 in the same manner.

	Column I	Column II	
1.	Johnston 12/26/74 659251	A. Johnson 12/23/74 659251 B. Johston 12/26/74 659251 C. Johnston 12/26/74 695251 D. Johnston 12/26/74 659251	1.____
2.	Allison 1/26/75 9939256	A. Allison 1/26/75 9939256 B. Alisson 1/26/75 9939256 C. Allison 1/26/76 9399256 D. Allison 1/26/75 9993356	2.____
3.	Farrell 2/12/75 361251	A. Farell 2/21/75 361251 B. Farrell 2/12/75 361251 C. Farrell 2/21/75 361251 D. Farrell 2/12/75 361151	3.____

4. Guerrero 4/28/72 105689
    A. Guererro 4/28/72 105689
    B. Guererro 4/28/72 105986
    C. Guererro 4/28/72 105869
    D. Guerrero 4/28/72 105689

    4.____

5. McDonnell 6/05/73 478215
    A. McDonnell 6/15/73 478215
    B. McDonnell 6/05/73 478215
    C. McDonnell 6/05/73 472815
    D. MacDonell 6/05/73 478215

    5.____

6. Shepard 3/31/71 075421
    A. Sheperd 3/31/71 075421
    B. Shepard 3/13/71 075421
    C. Shepard 3/31/71 075421
    D. Shepard 3/13/71 075241

    6.____

7. Russell 4/01/69 031429
    A. Russell 4/01/69 031429
    B. Russell 4/10/69 034129
    C. Russell 4/10/69 031429
    D. Russell 4/01/69 034129

    7.____

8. Phillips 10/16/68 961042
    A. Philipps 10/16/68 961042
    B. Phillips 10/16/68 960142
    C. Phillips 10/16/68 961042
    D. Philipps 10/16/68 916042

    8.____

9. Campbell 11/21/72 624856
    A. Campbell 11/21/72 624856
    B. Campbell 11/21/72 624586
    C. Campbell 11/21/72 624686
    D. Campbel   11/21/72 624856

    9.____

10. Patterson 9/18/71 76199176
    A. Patterson 9/18/72 76191976
    B. Patterson 9/18/71 76199176
    C. Patterson 9/18/72 76199176
    D. Patterson 9/18/71 76919176

    10.____

Questions 11-15.

DIRECTIONS: Questions 11 through 15 consist of groups of numbers and letters which you are to compare. For each question, you are to choose the option (A, B, C, or D) in Column I which EXACTLY matches the group of numbers and letters given in Column I.

SAMPLE QUESTION

Column I
B92466

Column II
A. B92644
B. B94266
C. A92466
D. B92466

The correct answer is D. Only Option D in Column II shows the group of numbers and letters EXACTLY as it appears in Column I. Now answer Questions 11 through 15 in the same manner.

	Column I	Column II	
11.	925AC5	A. 952CA5 B. 925AC5 C. 952AC5 D. 925CA6	11.____
12.	Y006925	A. Y060925 B. Y006295 C. Y006529 D. Y006925	12.____
13.	J236956	A. J236956 B. J326965 C. J239656 D. J932656	13.____
14.	AB6952	A. AB6952 B. AB9625 C. AB9652 D. AB6925	14.____
15.	X259361	A. X529361 B. X259631 C. X523961 D. X259361	15.____

Questions 16-25.

DIRECTIONS: Each of questions 16 through 25 consists of three lines of code letters and three lines of numbers. The numbers on each line should correspond with the code letters on the same line in accordance with the table below.

Code Letter	S	V	W	A	Q	M	X	E	G	K
Corresponding Number	0	1	2	3	4	5	5	7	8	9

On some of the lines, an error exists in the coding. Compare the letters and numbers in each question carefully. If you find an error or errors on:
    only one of the lines in the question, mark your answer A;
    any two lines in the question, mark your answer B;
    all three lines in the question, mark your answer C;
    none of the lines in the question, mark your answer D.

4 (#1)

SAMPLE QUESTION

WQGKSXG	2489068
XEKVQMA	6591453
KMAESXV	9527061

In the above sample, the first line is correct since each code letter listed has the correct corresponding number. On the second line, an error exists because code letter E should have the number 7 instead of the number 5. On the third line, an error exists because the code letter A should have the number 3 instead of the number 2. Since there are errors in two of the three lines, the correct answer is B. Now answer Questions 16 through 25 in the same manner.

16. SWQEKGA   0247983   16.____
      KEAVSXM   9731065
      SSAXGKQ   0036894

17. QAMKMVS   4259510   17.____
      MGGEASX   5897306
      KSWMKWS   9125920

18. WKXQWVE   2964217   18.____
      QKXXQVA   4966413
      AWMXGVS   3253810

19. GMMKASE   8559307   19.____
      AWVSKSW   3210902
      QAVSVGK   4310189

20. XGKQSMK   6894049   20.____
      QSVKEAS   4019730
      GSMXKMV   8057951

21. AEKMWSG   3195208   21.____
      MKQSVQK   5940149
      XGQAEVW   6843712

22. XGMKAVS   6858310   22.____
      SKMAWEQ   0953174
      GVMEQSA   8167403

23. VQSKAVE   1489317   23.____
      WQGKAEM   2489375
      MEGKAWQ   5689324

24. XMQVSKG   6541098   24.____
      QMEKEWS   4579720
      KMEVGKG   9571983

25. GKVAMEW   88912572   25._____
     AXMVKAE   3651937
     KWAGMAV   9238531

Questions 26-35.

DIRECTIONS: Each of Questions 26 through 35 consists of a column of figures. For each question, add the column of figures and choose the correct answer from the four choices given.

26. 5,665.43   26._____
     2,356.69
     6,447.24
     7,239.65

     A. 20,698.01   B. 21,709.01
     C. 21,718.01   D. 22,609.01

27. 817,209.55   27._____
     264,354.29
      82,368.76
     849,964.89

     A. 1,893.977.49   B. 1,989,988.39
     C. 2,009,077.39   D. 2,013,897.49

28. 156,366.89   28._____
     249,973.23
     823,229.49
      56,869.45

     A. 1,286,439.06   B. 1,287,521.06
     C. 1,297,539.06   D. 1,296,421.06

29.   23,422.15   29._____
     149,696.24
     238,377.53
      86,289.79
     505,533.63

     A. 989,229.34   B. 999,879.34
     C. 1,003,330.34   D. 1,023,329.34

30. 2,468,926.70
    656,842.28
      49,723.15
    832,369.59

    A. 3,218,062.72   B. 3,808,092.72
    C. 4,007,861.72   D. 4,818,192.72

30.____

31.   524,201.52
   7,775,678.51
   8,345,299.63
 40,628,898.08
 31,374,670.07

    A. 88,646,647.81   B. 88,646,747.91
    C. 88,648,647.91   D. 88,648,747.81

31.____

32. 6,824,829.40
   682,482.94
 5,542,015.27
   775,678.51
 7,732,507.25

    A. 21,557,513.37   B. 21,567,513.37
    C. 22,567,503.37   D. 22,567,513.37

32.____

33. 22,109,405.58
  6,097,093.43
  5,050,073.99
  8,118,050.05
  4,313,980.82

    A. 45,688,593.87   B. 45,688,603.87
    C. 45,689,593.87   D. 45,689,603.87

33.____

34. 79,324,114.19
 99,848,129.74
 43,331,653.31
 41,610,207.14

    A. 264,114,104.38   B. 264,114,114.38
    C. 265,114,114.38   D. 265,214,104.38

34.____

35. 33,729,653.94   35._____
     5,959,342.58
    26,052,715.47
     4,452,669.52
     7,079,953.59

    A. 76,374,334.10   B. 76,375,334.10
    C. 77,274,335.10   D. 77,275,335.10

Questions 36-40.

DIRECTIONS: Each of Questions 36 through 40 consists of a single number in Column I and four options in Column II. For each question, you are to choose the option (A, B, C, or D) in Column II which EXACTLY matches the number in Column I.

SAMPLE QUESTION

Column I   Column II
5965121   A. 5956121
                B. 5965121
                C. 5966121
                D. 5965211

The correct answer is B. Only Option B shows the number EXACTLY as it appears in Column I. Now answer Questions 36 through 40 in the same manner.

   Column I   Column II
36. 9643242   A. 9643242   36._____
                                   B. 9462342
                                   C. 9642442
                                   D. 9463242

37. 3572477   A. 3752477   37._____
                                   B. 3725477
                                   C. 3572477
                                   D. 3574277

38. 5276101   A. 5267101   38._____
                                   B. 5726011
                                   C. 5271601
                                   D. 5276101

39. 4469329   A. 4496329   39._____
                                   B. 4469329
                                   C. 4496239
                                   D. 4469239

40. 2326308	A. 2236308	40._____
	B. 2233608
	C. 2326308
	D. 2323608

KEY (CORRECT ANSWERS)

1.	D	11.	B	21.	A	31.	D
2.	A	12.	D	22.	C	32.	A
3.	B	13.	A	23.	B	33.	B
4.	D	14.	A	24.	D	34.	A
5.	B	15.	D	25.	A	35.	C
6.	C	16.	D	26.	B	36.	A
7.	A	17.	C	27.	D	37.	C
8.	C	18.	A	28.	A	38.	D
9.	A	19.	D	29.	C	39.	B
10.	B	20.	B	30.	C	40.	C

TEST 2

DIRECTIONS: Each question or incomplete statement is followed by several suggested answers or completions. Select the one that BEST answers the question or completes the statement. *PRINT THE LETTER OF THE CORRECT ANSWER IN THE SPACE AT THE RIGHT.*

Questions 1-5.

DIRECTIONS: Each of Questions 1 through 5 consists of a name and a dollar amount. In each question, the name and dollar amount in Column II should be an EXACT copy of the name and dollar amount in Column I. If there is:
    a mistake only in the name, mark your answer A;
    a mistake only in the dollar amount, mark your answer B;
    a mistake in both the name and the dollar amount, mark your answer C;
    no mistake in either the name or the dollar amount, mark your answer D.

SAMPLE QUESTION

Column I	Column II
George Peterson	George Petersson
$125.50	$125.50

Compare the name and dollar amount in Column II with the name and dollar amount in Column I. The name *Petersson* in Column II is spelled *Peterson* in Column I. The amount is the same in both columns. Since there is a mistake only in the name, the answer to the sample question is A. Now answer Questions 1 through 5 in the same manner.

	Column I	Column II	
1.	Susanne Shultz $3440	Susanne Schultz $3440	1.____
2.	Anibal P. Contrucci $2121.61	Anibel P. Contrucci $2112.61	2.____
3.	Eugenio Mendoza $12.45	Eugenio Mendozza $12.45	3.____
4.	Maurice Gluckstadt $4297	Maurice Gluckstadt $4297	4.____
5.	John Pampellonne $4656.94	John Pammpellonne $4566.94	5.____

Questions 6-11.

DIRECTIONS: Each of Questions 6 through 11 consist of a set of names and addresses, which you are to compare. In each question, the name and addresses in Column II should be an EXACT copy of the name and address in Column I. If there is:
- a mistake only in the name, mark your answer A;
- a mistake only in the address, mark your answer B;
- a mistake in both the name and address, mark your answer C;
- no mistake in either the name or address, mark your answer D.

SAMPLE QUESTION

Column I
Michael Filbert
456 Reade Street
New York, N.Y. 10013

Column II
Michael Filbert
645 Reade Street
New York, N.Y. 10013

Since there is a mistake only in the address (the street number should be 456 instead of 645), the answer to the sample question is B. Now answer Questions 6 through 11 in the same manner.

	Column I	Column II	
6.	Hilda Goettelmann 55 Lenox Rd. Brooklyn, N.Y. 11226	Hilda Goettelman 55 Lenox Ave. Brooklyn, N.Y. 11226	6.____
7.	Arthur Sherman 2522 Batchelder St. Brooklyn, N.Y. 11235	Arthur Sharman 2522 Batcheder St. Brooklyn, N.Y. 11253	7.____
8.	Ralph Barnett 300 West 28 Street New York, New York 10001	Ralph Barnett 300 West 28 Street New York, New York 10001	8.____
9.	George Goodwin 135 Palmer Avenue Staten Island, New York 10302	George Godwin 135 Palmer Avenue Staten Island, New York 10302	9.____
10.	Alonso Ramirez 232 West 79 Street New York, N.Y. 10024	Alonso Ramirez 223 West 79 Street New York, N.Y. 10024	10.____
11.	Cynthia Graham 149-34 83 Street Howard Beach, N.Y. 11414	Cynthia Graham 149-35 83 Street Howard Beach, N.Y. 11414	11.____

Questions 12-20.

DIRECTIONS: Questions 12 through 20 are problems in subtraction. For each question do the subtraction and select your answer from the four choices given.

12. 232,921.85
    -179,587.68

    A. 52,433.17   B. 52,434.17
    C. 53,334.17   D. 53,343,17

    12.____

13. 5,531,876.29
    -3,897,158.36

    A. 1,634,717.93   B. 1,644,718.93
    C. 1,734,717.93   D. 1,7234,718.93

    13.____

14. 1,482,658.22
    -937,925.76

    A. 544,633.46   B. 544,732.46
    C. 545,632.46   D. 545,732.46

    14.____

15. 937,828.17
    -259,673.88

    A. 678,154.29   B. 679,154.29
    C. 688,155.39   D. 699,155.39

    15.____

16. 760,412.38
    -263,465.95

    A. 496,046.43   B. 496,946.43
    C. 496,956.43   D. 497,046.43

    16.____

17. 3,203,902.26
    -2,933,087.96

    A. 260,814.30   B. 269,824.30
    C. 270,814.30   D. 270,824.30

    17.____

18. 1,023,468.71
    -934,678.88

    A. 88,780.83   B. 88,789.83
    C. 88,880.83   D. 88,889.83

    18.____

4 (#2)

19. 831,549.47
    -772,814.78

    A. 58,734.69   B. 58,834.69
    C. 59,735.69   D. 59,834.69

19.____

20. 6,306,181.74
    -3,617,376.99

    A. 2,687,904.99   B. 2,688,904.99
    C. 2,689,804.99   D. 2,799,905.99

20.____

Questions 21-30.

DIRECTIONS: Each of Questions 21 through 30 consists of three lines of code letters and three lines of numbers. The numbers on each line should correspond with the code letters on the same line in accordance with the table below.

Code Letter	J	U	B	T	Y	D	K	R	L	P
Corresponding Number	0	1	2	3	4	5	5	7	8	9

On some of the lines, an error exists in the coding. Compare the letters and numbers in each question carefully. If you find an error or errors on:
    only *one* of the lines in the question, mark your answer A;
    any *two* lines in the question, mark your answer B;
    all *three* lines in the question, mark your answer C;
    none of the lines in the question, mark your answer D.

SAMPLE QUESTION

    BJRPYUR   2079417
    DTBPYKJ   5328460
    YKLDBLT   4685283

In the above sample, the first line is correct since each code letter listed has the correct corresponding number. On the second line, an error exists because code letter P should have the number 9 instead of the number 8. The third line is correct since each code letter listed has the correct corresponding number. Since there is an error in *one* of the three lines, the correct answer is A. Now answer Questions 21 through 30 in the same manner.

21. BYPDTJL   2495308
    PLRDTJU   9815301
    DTJRYLK   5207486

21.____

22. RPBYRJK   7934706
    PKTYLBU   9624821
    KDLPJYR   6489047

22.____

23.	TPYBUJR BYRKPTU DUKPYDL	3942107 2476931 5169458	23.____
24.	KBYDLPL BLRKBRU JTULDYB	6345898 2876261 0318542	24.____
25.	LDPYDKR BDKDRJL BDRPLUJ	8594567 2565708 2679810	25.____
26.	PLRLBPU LPYKRDJ TDKPDTR	9858291 88936750 3569527	26.____
27.	RKURPBY RYUKPTJ RTKPTJD	7617924 7426930 7369305	27.____
28.	DYKPBJT KLPJBTL TKPLBJP	5469203 6890238 3698209	28.____
29.	BTPRJYL LDKUTYR YDBLRPJ	2397148 8561347 4528190	29.____
30.	ULPBKYT KPDTRBJ YLKJPTB	1892643 6953720 4860932	30.____

KEY (CORRECT ANSWERS)

1.	A	11.	D	21.	B
2.	C	12.	C	22.	C
3.	A	13.	A	23.	D
4.	D	14.	B	24.	B
5.	C	15.	A	25.	A
6.	C	16.	B	26.	C
7.	C	17.	C	27.	A
8.	D	18.	B	28.	D
9.	A	19.	A	29.	B
10.	B	20.	B	30.	D

CLERICAL ABILITIES
EXAMINATION SECTION
TEST 1

DIRECTIONS: Each question or incomplete statement is followed by several suggested answers or completions. Select the one that BEST answers the question or completes the statement. *PRINT THE LETTER OF THE CORRECT ANSWER IN THE SPACE AT THE RIGHT.*

Questions 1-4.

DIRECTIONS: Questions 1 through 4 are to be answered on the basis of the information given below.

    The most commonly used filing system and the one that is easiest to learn is alphabetical filing. This involves putting records in an A to Z order, according to the letters of the alphabet. The name of a person is filed by using the following order: first, the surname or last name; second, the first name; third, the middle name or middle initial. For example, *Henry C. Young* is filed under *Y* and thereafter under *Young, Henry C.* The name of a company is filed in the same way. For example, *Long Cabinet Co.* is filed under *L* while *John T. Long Cabinet Co.* is filed under *L* and thereafter under *Long, John T. Cabinet Co.*

1. The one of the following which lists the names of persons in the CORRECT alphabetical order is:
   A. Mary Carrie, Helen Carrol, James Carson, John Carter
   B. James Carson, Mary Carrie, John Carter, Helen Carrol
   C. Helen Carrol, James Carson, John Carter, Mary Carrie
   D. John Carter, Helen Carrol, Mary Carrie, James Carson

2. The one of the following which lists the names of persons in the CORRECT alphabetical order is:
   A. Jones, John C.; Jones, John A.; Jones, John P.; Jones, John K.
   B. Jones, John P.; Jones, John K.; Jones, John C.; Jones, John A.
   C. Jones, John A.; Jones, John C.; Jones, John K.; Jones, John P.
   D. Jones, John K.; Jones, John C.; Jones, John A.; Jones, John P.

3. The one of the following which lists the names of the companies in the CORRECT alphabetical order is:
   A. Blane Co., Blake Co., Block Co., Blear Co.
   B. Blake Co., Blane Co., Blear Co., Block Co.
   C. Block Co., Blear Co., Blane Co., Blake Co.
   D. Blear Co., Blake Co., Blane Co., Block Co.

1.____

2.____

3.____

4. You are to return to the file an index card on *Barry C. Wayne Materials and Supplies Co.*
Of the following, the CORRECT alphabetical group that you should return the index card to is
   A. A to G   B. H to M   C. N to S   D. T to Z

Questions 5-10.

DIRECTIONS: In each of Questions 5 through 10, the names of four people are given. For each question, choose as your answer the one of the four names given which should be filed FIRST according to the usual system of alphabetical filing of names, as described in the following paragraph.

In filing names, you must start with the last name. Names are filed in order of the first letter of the last name, then the second letter, etc. Therefore, BAILY would be filed before BROWN, which would be filed before COLT. A name with fewer letters of the same type comes first, i.e., Smith before Smithe. If the last names are the same, the names are filed alphabetically by the first name. If the first name is an initial, a name with an initial would come before a first name that starts with the same letter as the initial. Therefore, I. BROWN would come before IRA BROWN. Finally, if both last name and first name are the same, the name would be filed alphabetically by the middle name, once again an initial coming before a middle name which starts with the same letter as the initial. If there is no middle name at all, the name would come before those with middle initials or names.

SAMPLE QUESTION: A. Lester Daniels
                   B. William Dancer
                   C. Nathan Danzig
                   D. Dan Lester

The last names beginning with D are filed before the last name beginning with L. Since DANIELS, DANCER, and DANZIG all begin with the same three letters, you must look at the fourth letter of the last name to determine which name should be filed first. C comes before I or Z in the alphabet, so DANCER is filed before DANIELS or DANZIG. Therefore, the answer to the above sample question is B.

5. A. Scott Biala
   B. Mary Byala
   C. Martin Baylor
   D. Francis Bauer

6. A. Howard J. Black
   B. Howard Black
   C. J. Howard Black
   D. John H. Black

7. A. Theodora Garth Kingston
   B. Theadore Barth Kingston
   C. Thomas Kingston
   D. Thomas T. Kingston

8. A. Paulette Mary Huerta
    B. Paul M. Huerta
    C. Paulette L. Huerta
    D. Peter A. Huerta

9. A. Martha Hunt Morgan
    B. Martin Hunt Morgan
    C. Mary H. Morgan
    D. Martine H. Morgan

10. A. James T. Meerschaum
    B. James M. Mershum
    C. James F. Mearshaum
    D. James N. Meshum

Questions 11-14.

DIRECTIONS: Questions 11 through 14 are to be answered SOLELY on the basis of the following information.

You are required to file various documents in file drawers which are labeled according to the following pattern:

DOCUMENTS

MEMOS		LETTERS	
File	Subject	File	Subject
84PM1	(A-L)	84PC1	(A-L)
84PM2	(M-Z)	84PC2	(M-Z)

REPORTS		INQUIRIES	
File	Subject	File	Subject
84PR1	(A-L)	84PQ1	(A-L)
84PR2	(M-Z)	84PQ2	(M-Z)

11. A letter dealing with a burglary should be filed in the drawer labeled
    A. 84PM1   B. 84PC1   C. 84PR1   D. 84PQ2

12. A report on Statistics should be found in the drawer labeled
    A. 84PM1   B. 84PC2   C. 84PR2   D. 84PQS

13. An inquiry is received about parade permit procedures. It should be filed in the drawer labeled
    A. 84PM2   B. 84PC1   C. 84PR1   D. 84PQ2

14. A police officer has a question about a robbery report you filed. You should pull this file from the drawer labeled
    A. 84PM1   B. 84PM2   C. 84PR1   D. 84PR2

Questions 15-22.

DIRECTIONS: Each of Questions 15 through 22 consists of four or six numbered names. For each question, choose the option (A, B, C, or D) which indicates the order in which the names should be filed in accordance with the following filing instructions:
- File alphabetically according to last name, then first name, then middle initial.
- File according to each successive letter within a name.
- When comparing two names in which the letters in the longer name are identical to the corresponding letters in the shorter name, the shorter name is filed first.
- When the last names are the same, initials are always filed before names beginning with the same letter.

15. I. Ralph Robinson
    II. Alfred Ross
    III. Luis Robles
    IV. James Roberts

    The CORRECT filing sequence for the above names should be
    A. IV, II, I, III   B. I, IV, III, II   C. III, IV, I, II   D. IV, I, III, II

16. I. Irwin Goodwin
    II. Inez Gonzalez
    III. Irene Goodman
    IV. Ira S. Goodwin
    V. Ruth I. Goldstein
    VI. M.B. Goodman

    The CORRECT filing sequence for the above names should be
    A. V, II, I, IV, III, VI
    B. V, II, VI, III, IV, I
    C. V, II, III, VI, IV, I
    D. V, II, III, VI, I, IV

17. I. George Allan
    II. Gregory Allen
    III. Gary Allen
    IV. George Allen

    The CORRECT filing sequence for the above names should be
    A. IV, III, I, II   B. I, IV, II, III   C. III, IV, I, II   D. I, III, IV, II

5 (#1)

18. I. Simon Kauffman
     II. Leo Kaufman
     III. Robert Kaufmann
     IV. Paul Kauffmann

     The CORRECT filing sequence for the above names should be
     A. I, IV, II, III   B. II, IV, III, I   C. III, II, IV, I   D. I, II, III, IV

19. I. Roberta Williams
     II. Robin Wilson
     III. Roberta Wilson
     IV. Robin Williams

     The CORRECT filing sequence for the above names should be
     A. III, II, IV, I   B. I, IV, III, II   C. I, II, III, IV   D. III, I, II, IV

20. I. Lawrence Shultz
     II. Albert Schultz
     III. Theodore Schwartz
     IV. Thomas Schwarz
     V. Alvin Schultz
     VI. Leonard Shultz

     The CORRECT filing sequence for the above names should be
     A. II, V, III, IV, I, VI   B. IV, III, V, I, II, VI
     C. II, V, I, VI, III, IV   D. I, VI, II, V, III, IV

21. I. McArdle
     II. Mayer
     III. Maletz
     IV. McNiff
     V. Meyer
     VI. MacMahon

     The CORRECT filing sequence for the above names should be
     A. I, IV, VI, III, II, V   B. II, I, IV, VI, III, V
     C. VI, III, II, I, IV, V   D. VI, III, II, V, I, IV

22. I. Jack E. Johnson
     II. R.H. Jackson
     III. Bertha Jackson
     IV. J.T. Johnson
     V. Ann Johns
     VI. John Jacobs

     The CORRECT filing sequence for the above names should be
     A. II, III, VI, V, IV, I   B. III, II, VI, V, IV, I
     C. VI, II, III, I, V, IV   D. III, II, VI, IV, V, I

Questions 23-30.

DIRECTIONS: The code table below shows 10 letters with matching numbers. For each question, there are three sets of letters. Each set of letters is followed by a set of numbers which may or may not match their correct letter according to the code table. For each question, check all three sets of letters and numbers and mark your answer:
  A. if no pairs are correctly matched
  B. if only one pair is correctly matched
  C. if only two pairs are correctly matched
  D. if all three pairs are correctly matched

CODE TABLE

T	M	V	D	S	P	R	G	B	H
1	2	3	4	5	6	7	8	9	0

SAMPLE QUESTION: TMVDSP – 123456
RGBHTM – 789011
DSPRGB – 256789

In the sample question above, the first set of numbers correctly match its set of letters. But the second and third pairs contain mistakes. In the second pair, M is correctly matched with number 1. According to the code table, letter M should be correctly matched with number 2. In the third pair, the letter D is incorrectly matched with number 2. According to the code table, letter D should be correctly matched with number 4. Since only one of the pairs is correctly matched, the answer to this sample question is B.

23. RSBMRM – 759262
    GDSRVH – 845730
    VDBRTM - 349713   23.____

24. TGVSDR – 183247
    SMHRDP – 520647
    TRMHSR - 172057   24.____

25. DSPRGM – 456782
    MVDBHT – 234902
    HPMDBT - 062491   25.____

26. BVPTRD – 936184
    GDPHMB – 807029
    GMRHMV - 827032   26.____

27. MGVRSH – 283750
    TRDMBS – 174295
    SPRMGV - 567283   27.____

28. SGBSDM – 489542 28.____
    MGHPTM – 290612
    MPBMHT - 269301

29. TDPBHM – 146902 29.____
    VPBMRS – 369275
    GDMBHM - 842902

30. MVPTBV – 236194 30.____
    PDRTMB – 47128
    BGTMSM - 981232

KEY (CORRECT ANSWERS)

1.	A	11.	B	21.	C
2.	C	12.	C	22.	B
3.	B	13.	D	23.	B
4.	D	14.	D	24.	B
5.	D	15.	D	25.	C
6.	B	16.	C	26.	A
7.	B	17.	D	27.	D
8.	B	18.	A	28.	A
9.	A	19.	B	29.	D
10.	C	20.	A	30.	A

TEST 2

DIRECTIONS: Each question or incomplete statement is followed by several suggested answers or completions. Select the one that BEST answers the question or completes the statement. *PRINT THE LETTER OF THE CORRECT ANSWER IN THE SPACE AT THE RIGHT.*

Questions 1-10.

DIRECTIONS: Questions 1 through 10 each consists of two columns, each containing four lines of names, numbers and/or addresses. For each question, compare the lines in Column I with the lines in Column II to see if they match exactly, and mark your answer A, B, C, or D, according to the following instructions:
    A. all four lines match exactly
    B. only three lines match exactly
    C. only two lines match exactly
    D. only one line matches exactly

<u>COLUMN I</u>   <u>COLUMN II</u>

1.   I.   Earl Hodgson   Earl Hodgson   1.____
     II.   1409870   1408970
     III.   Shore Ave.   Schore Ave.
     IV.   Macon Rd.   Macon Rd.

2.   I.   9671485   9671485   2.____
     II.   470 Astor Court   470 Astor Court
     III.   Halprin, Phillip   Halperin, Phillip
     IV.   Frank D. Poliseo   Frank D. Poliseo

3.   I.   Tandem Associates   Tandom Associates   3.____
     II.   144-17 Northern Blvd.   144-17 Northern Blvd.
     III.   Alberta Forchi   Albert Forchi
     IV.   Kings Park, NY 10751   Kings Point, NY 10751

4.   I.   Bertha C. McCormack   Bertha C. McCormack   4.____
     II.   Clayton, MO   Clayton, MO
     III.   976-4242   976-4242
     IV.   New City, NY 10951   New City, NY 10951

5.   I.   George C. Morill   George C. Morrill   5.____
     II.   Columbia, SC 29201   Columbia, SD 29201
     III.   Louis Ingham   Louis Ingham
     IV.   3406 Forest Ave.   3406 Forest Ave.

6.   I.   506 S. Elliott Pl.   506 S. Elliott Pl.   6.____
     II.   Herbert Hall   Hurbert Hall
     III.   4712 Rockaway Pkway   4712 Rockaway Pkway
     IV.   169 E. 7 St.   169 E. 7 St.

7. I.   345 Park Ave.   345 Park Pl.   7.____
    II. Colman Oven Corp.   Coleman Oven Corp.
    III. Robert Conte   Robert Conti
    IV. 6179846   6179846

8. I.   Grigori Schierber   Grigori Schierber   8.____
    II. Des Moines, Iowa   Des Moines, Iowa
    III. Gouverneur Hospital   Gouverneur Hospital
    IV. 91-35 Cresskill Pl.   91-35 Cresskill Pl.

9. I.   Jeffery Janssen   Jeffrey Janssen   9.____
    II. 8041071   8041071
    III. 40 Rockefeller Plaza   40 Rockafeller Plaza
    IV. 407 6 St.   406 7 St.

10. I.   5971996   5871996   10.____
    II. 3113 Knickerbocker Ave.   31123 Knickerbocker Ave.
    III. 8434 Boston Post Rd.   8424 Boston Post Rd.
    IV. Penn Station   Penn Station

Questions 11-14.

DIRECTIONS: Questions 11 through 14 are to be answered by looking at the four groups of names and addresses listed below (I, II, III, and IV), and then finding out the number of groups that have their corresponding numbered lies exactly the same.

	GROUP I	GROUP II
Line 1.	Richmond General Hospital	Richman General Hospital
Line 2.	Geriatric Clinic	Geriatric Clinic
Line 3.	3975 Paerdegat St.	3975 Peardegat St.
Line 4.	Loudonville, New York 11538	Londonville, New York 11538

	GROUP III	GROUP IV
Line 1.	Richmond General Hospital	Richmend General Hospital
Line 2.	Geriatric Clinic	Geriatric Clinic
Line 3.	3795 Paerdegat St.	3975 Paerdegat St.
Line 4.	Loudonville, New York 11358	Loudonville, New York 11538

1. In how many groups is line one exactly the same?   11.____
    A. Two   B. Three   C. Four   D. None

12. In how many groups is line two exactly the same?   12.____
    A. Two   B. Three   C. Four   D. None

13. In how many groups is line three exactly the same?   13.____
    A. Two   B. Three   C. Four   D. None

14. In how many groups is line four exactly the same? 14.____
    A. Two   B. Three   C. Four   D. None

Questions 15-18.

DIRECTIONS: Each of Questions 15 through 18 has two lists of names and addresses. Each list contains three sets of names and addresses. Check each of the three sets in the list on the right to see if they are the same as the corresponding set in the list on the left. Mark your answers:
- A. if none of the sets in the right list are the same as those in the left list
- B. if only one of the sets in the right list is the same as those in the left list
- C. if only two of the sets in the right list are the same as those in the left list
- D. if all three sets in the right list are the same as those in the left list

15. Mary T. Berlinger   Mary T. Berlinger   15.____
    2351 Hampton St.   2351 Hampton St.
    Monsey, N.Y. 20117   Monsey, N.Y. 20117

    Eduardo Benes   Eduardo Benes
    483 Kingston Avenue   473 Kingston Avenue
    Central Islip, N.Y. 11734   Central Islip, N.Y. 11734

    Alan Carrington Fuchs   Alan Carrington Fuchs
    17 Gnarled Hollow Road   17 Gnarled Hollow Road
    Los Angeles, CA 91635   Los Angeles, CA 91685

16. David John Jacobson   David John Jacobson   16.____
    178 34 St. Apt. 4C   178 53 St. Apt. 4C
    New York, N.Y. 00927   New York, N.Y. 00927

    Ann-Marie Calonella   Ann-Marie Calonella
    7243 South Ridge Blvd.   7243 South Ridge Blvd.
    Bakersfield, CA 96714   Bakersfield, CA 96714

    Pauline M. Thompson   Pauline M. Thomson
    872 Linden Ave.   872 Linden Ave.
    Houston, Texas 70321   Houston, Texas 70321

17. Chester LeRoy Masterton   Chester LeRoy Masterson   17.____
    152 Lacy Rd.   152 Lacy Rd.
    Kankakee, Ill. 54532   Kankakee, Ill. 54532

    William Maloney   William Maloney
    S. LaCrosse Pla.   S. LaCross Pla.
    Wausau, Wisconsin 52136   Wausau, Wisconsin 52146

    Cynthia V. Barnes   Cynthia V. Barnes
    16 Pines Rd.   16 Pines Rd.
    Greenpoint, Miss. 20376   Greenpoint,, Miss. 20376

4 (#2)

18. Marcel Jean Frontenac   Marcel Jean Frontenac   18._____
    8 Burton On The Water   6 Burton On The Water
    Calender, Me. 01471   Calender, Me. 01471

    J. Scott Marsden   J. Scott Marsden
    174 S. Tipton St.   174 Tipton St.
    Cleveland, Ohio   Cleveland, Ohio

    Lawrence T. Haney   Lawrence T. Haney
    171 McDonough St.   171 McDonough St.
    Decatur, Ga. 31304   Decatur, Ga. 31304

Questions 19-26.

DIRECTIONS: Each of Questions 19 through 26 has two lists of numbers. Each list contains three sets of numbers. Check each of the three sets in the list on the right to see if they are the same as the corresponding set in the list on the left. Mark your answers:
- A. if none of the sets in the right list are the same as those in the left list
- B. if only one of the sets in the right list is the same as those in the left list
- C. if only two of the sets in the right list are the same as those in the left list
- D. if all three sets in the right list are the same as those in the left lists

19. 7354183476   7354983476   19._____
    4474747744   4474747774
    5791430231   57914302311

20. 7143592185   7143892185   20._____
    8344517699   8344518699
    9178531263   9178531263

21. 2572114731   257214731   21._____
    8806835476   8806835476
    8255831246   8255831246

22. 331476853821   331476858621   22._____
    6976658532996   6976655832996
    3766042113715   3766042113745

23. 8806663315   88066633115   23._____
    74477138449   74477138449
    211756663666   211756663666

24. 990006966996   99000696996   24.____
    53022219743   53022219843
    4171171117717   4171171177717

25. 24400222433004   24400222433004   25.____
    5300030055000355   5300030055500355
    20000075532002022   20000075532002022

26. 6111666406600011116   61116664066001116   26.____
    7111300117001100733   7111300117001100733
    26666446664476518   26666446664476518

Questions 27-30.

DIRECTIONS: Questions 27 through 30 are to be answered by picking the answer which is in the correct numerical order, from the lowest number to the highest number, in each question.

27. A. 44533, 44518, 44516, 44547   27.____
    B. 44516, 44518, 44533, 44547
    C. 44547, 44533, 44518, 44516
    D. 44518, 44516, 44547, 44533

28. A. 95587, 95593, 95601, 95620   28.____
    B. 95601, 95620, 95587, 95593
    C. 95593, 95587, 95601. 95620
    D. 95620, 95601, 95593, 95587

29. A. 232212, 232208, 232232, 232223   29.____
    B. 232208, 232223, 232212, 232232
    C. 232208, 232212, 232223, 232232
    D. 232223, 232232, 232208, 232208

30. A. 113419, 113521, 113462, 113462   30.____
    B. 113588, 113462, 113521, 113419
    C. 113521, 113588, 113419, 113462
    D. 113419, 113462, 113521, 113588

KEY (CORRECT ANSWERS)

1. C	11. A	21. C
2. B	12. C	22. A
3. D	13. A	23. D
4. A	14. A	24. A
5. C	15. C	25. C
6. B	16. B	26. C
7. D	17. B	27. B
8. A	18. B	28. A
9. D	19. B	29. C
10. C	20. B	30. D

EXAMINATION SECTION
TEST 1

DIRECTIONS: Each question or incomplete statement is followed by several suggested answers or completions. Select the one that BEST answers the question or completes the statement. *PRINT THE LETTER OF THE CORRECT ANSWER IN THE SPACE AT THE RIGHT.*

Questions 1-3
For questions 1 through 3, there is a name or code provided along with four other names or codes listed in alphabetical/numerical order. Find the correct space for the given name or code so that it will be in proper order with the rest of the list.

1. Roggen, Sam   1.____

   A. _
   Rogers, Arthur L
   B. _
   Roghani, Fada
   C. _
   Rogovin, H.T.
   D. _
   Rogowski, Marie R.
   E. _

2. 05076012   2.____

   A. _
   05076004
   B. _
   05076007
   C. _
   05076010
   D. _
   05076021
   E. _

3. CBA-1875   3.____

   A. _
   CAA-1720
   B. _
   CAB-1819
   C. _
   CAC-1804
   D. _
   CAD-1402
   E. _

Questions 4-8
Questions 4 through 8 require you to compare names, addresses or codes. In each line below there are three items that are very much alike. Compare the three and answer as follows:

2 (#1)

Answer "A" if all three are exactly alike;
Answer "B" if only the FIRST and SECOND items are exactly alike;
Answer "C" if only the FIRST and THIRD items are exactly alike;
Answer "D" if only the SECOND AND THIRD items are exactly alike;
Answer "E" if all three names are different.

4. Helene Bedell   Helene Beddell   Helene Beddell   4.___

5. FT. Wedemeyer   FT. Wedemeyer   FT. Wedmeyer   5.___

6. 3214 W. Beaumont St. 3214 W. Beaumount St. 3214 Beaumont St.   6.___

7. BC3105T-5   BC3015T-5   BC3105T-5   7.___

8. 4460327   4460327   4460327   8.___

For questions 9 through 11, find the correct spelling of the word and write the correct letter in the space at the right.

9. A. accomodate   B. acommodate   9.___
    C. accommadate   D. none of the above

10. A. manageble   B. manageable   10.___
    C. manegeable   D. none of the above

11. A. reccommend   B. recommend   11.___
    C. recammend   D. none of the above

12. 32 + 26 =   12.___

    A. 69
    B. 59
    C. 58
    D. 54
    E. none of the above

13. 57-15 =   13.___

    A. 72
    B. 62
    C. 54
    D. 44
    E. none of the above

14. 23x7 =   14.___

    A. 164
    B. 161
    C. 154
    D. 141
    E. none of the above

15. 160/5 =   15.___

    A. 32

B. 30
C. 25
D. 21
E. none of the above

16. 17.8 + 13.3 =   16._____

   A. 30.1
   B. 31.0
   C. 31.1
   D. 33.3

Questions 17-19

Questions 17 through 19 test the ability to follow instructions. Following the directions in each item will lead you to identify or create a specific letter-number combination. Next, use the "Look-Up Table" to find the letter that corresponds with your letter-number combination. Mark this letter in the space at the right.

For example, if the combination is "P1," the answer would be "A" because this is the letter indicated in the box where "P" and "1" meet in the table.

LOOK-UP TABLE					
	P	Q	R	S	T
1	A	B	C	D	E
2	B	C	D	E	A
3	C	D	E	A	B
4	D	E	A	B	C
5	E	A	B	C	D
6-	A	B	C	D	E
7	B	C	D	E	A
8	C	D	E	A	B
9	D	E	A	B	C
10	E	A	B	C	D

17. Look at the letter-number combinations below. Draw a circle around the third combina-   17._____
    tion from the left. Write that letter-number combination in this space: _____
       T1   S5   P2   Q5   P5   R2

18. Draw a line under each letter that appears only once in the line. Write the letter "Q" and   18._____
    the number of lines you drew here: _____
       S T Q T Q P T Q

19. Look again at the line of letters in question 16. Draw a circle around each "Q." Write the   19._____
    letter that appears at the beginning of the line and the number of circles you drew here:

    _____

20. Select the sentence which is MOST APPROPRIATE with respect to grammar, usage and   20._____
    punctuation suitable for a formal letter or report:

    A. Major repairs has caused the cafeteria to be closed until late October.
    B. The cafeteria will be closed until late October on account of major repairs.

C. The cafeteria will be closed for major repairs until late October.
D. The closing of the cafeteria until late October due to the completion of major repairs.

In questions 21 through 23, identify the most similar meaning to the highlighted word:

21. The staff was **amazed** by the news.

    A. pleased
    B. surprised
    C. saddened
    D. relieved

22. Please **delete** the second paragraph.

    A. retype
    B. reread
    C. revise
    D. remove

23. Did you **duplicate** the information as written?

    A. type
    B. copy
    C. remember
    D. understand

24. "It is a simple matter to find and correct the errors made by a typist, but often a file clerk's errors are not discovered until something which is needed cannot be found. For this reason, the work of every file clerk should be checked at regular intervals."
The paragraph BEST supports the statement that filing

    A. may contain errors that are not immediately noticeable
    B. should be organized by typists rather than file clerks
    C. is a more difficult process than typing
    D. should be checked for errors more frequently than typing

25. "The most efficient method for performing a task is not always easily determined. That which is economical in terms of time must be carefully distinguished from that which is economical in terms of expended energy. In short, the quickest method may require a degree of physical effort that may be neither essential nor desirable." The paragraph BEST supports the statement that

    A. it is more efficient to perform a task slowly than rapidly
    B. skill in performing a task should not be acquired at the expense of time
    C. the most efficient execution of a task is not always the one done in the shortest time
    D. energy and time cannot both be considered in the performance of a single task

KEY (CORRECT ANSWERS)

1.	B	11.	B
2.	D	12.	C
3.	E	13.	E
4.	D	14.	B
5.	B	15.	A
6.	E	16.	C
7.	C	17.	B
8.	A	18.	C
9.	D	19.	A
10.	B	20.	C

21. B
22. D
23. B
24. A
25. C

FILING

EXAMINATION SECTION
TEST 1

DIRECTIONS: For each of the following, you are given a name above and three other names in alphabetical order below. The letters A, B, C, and D stand for spaces where you could file the name. Find the CORRECT space for the name given above so that it will be in alphabetical order with the names below it. The letter that stands for that space is the answer to the question.

1. CURRAN, THOMAS
   A CURLEY, MARY B CURR, SAMUEL C CURREN, KATIE D

   1._____

2. KAPLIN, EDWIN
   A KAPLEN, MICHAEL B KAPLIN, JULIA C KAPLON, DAVID D

   2._____

3. PENSKY, LEONA
   A PENSLER, SANDY B PENSLEY, JOEL C PENSLEY, JOSEPH D

   3._____

4. ROWEN, MARCIA
   A ROWEN, CHRISTOPHER B ROWEN, LOUIS C ROWEN, MARTIN D

   4._____

5. FOSTER, GRACE
   A FOSS, EARL B FOSSE, NICHOLE C FOSTER, KEITH D

   5._____

6. KO, FAI
   A KO, HOK B KO, HUNG-FAI C KO, HYUN JUNG D

   6._____

7. MICHALIK, ANTHONY
   A MICHALIC, GARY B MICHALIS, HELEN C MICHALK, KLAUS D

   7._____

8. MINTZ, JUDITH
   A MINTZ, JAKE B MINTZ, JAMES C MINTZ, JULIUS D

   8._____

9. POWERS, ANN
   A POUST, THERESE B POWELL, LUTHER C POWER, RACHEL D

   9._____

10. PRACTICAL STUDIO, INC.
    A PRACTICAL PUBLISHING B PRACTICE DEVELOPMENT C PRACTICE SERVICE CORP. D

    10._____

11. SHERWIN, ROBERTA
    A SHERWIN, RAUL B SHERWIN, RICHARD C SHERWIN, ROBERT D

    11._____

12. JACOBSEN, JENNIFER
    A JACOBSON, PETER B JACOBY, JACK C JACOVITZ, GAIL D

    12._____

13. BLEINHEIM, GLORIA
    A BLELOCK, JULIA B BLENCOWE, FRED C BLENMAN, ANTHONY D

    13._____

14. FIRST STERLING CORP. 14.____
    A FIRST STATE PRODUCTS B FIRST STEP INC. C FIRST STOP CORP. D

15. VICKERS, GEORGE 15.____
    A VICHEY, LOUIS B VICHI, MARIO C VICKI, SUSAN D

16. STEIN, DAVID 16.____
    A STEIN, CRAIG B STEIN, DANIEL C STEIN, DEBORAH D

17. IGLESIAS, BERNADETTE 17.____
    A IGER, MARTIN B IGLEHEART, PHYLICIA C IGLEWSKI, RICHARD D

18. IDEAL ROOFING CORP. 18.____
    A IDEAL REPRODUCTION B IDEAL RESTAURANT C IDEAL RUBBER PRODUCTS D

19. TODARO, JOSEPH 19.____
    A TODD, ANNE B TODE, WALLY C TODMAN, JUDITH D

20. WILKERSON, RUTH 20.____
    A WILKENS, FRANK B WILKES, BARRY C WILKIE, JANE D

21. HUGHES, MARY 21.____
    A HUGHES, MANUEL B HUGHES, MARGARET C HUGHES, MARTHA D

22. GODWIN, JAMES 22.____
    A GODFREY, SONDRA B GODMAN, GABRIEL C GODREAU, ROBERT D

23. NACHMAN, DAVID 23.____
    A NACHT, JAMES B NACK, SAUL C NACKENSON, LORI D

24. CASPER, LAURENCE 24.____
    A CASPER, LEONARD B CASPER, LESTER C CASPER, LINDA D

25. CULEN, ELLEN 25.____
    A CULHANE, JOHN B CULICHI, RADU C CULIN, TERRY D

KEY (CORRECT ANSWERS)

1.	C	11.	D
2.	B	12.	A
3.	A	13.	A
4.	C	14.	C
5.	C	15.	C
6.	A	16.	C
7.	B	17.	C
8.	C	18.	C
9.	D	19.	A
10.	B	20.	B
21.	D		
22.	D		
23.	A		
24.	A		
25.	A		

TEST 2

DIRECTIONS: For each of the following, you are given a name above and three other names in alphabetical order below. The letters A, B, C, and D stand for spaces where you could file the name. Find the CORRECT space for the name given above so that it will be in alphabetical order with the names below it. The letter that stands for that space is the answer to the question.

1. HARMAN, HENRY
   A HARLEY, LILLIAN B HARMER, RALPH C HARMON, CECIL D   1._____

2. MANNING, JOHNSON
   A MANNING, JAMES B MANNING, JEROME C MANNING, JOHN D   2._____

3. NOGUCHI, JANICE
   A NOEL, WALTER B NOGUET, DANIELLE C NOH, DAVID D   3._____

4. PARRON, ALFONSE
   A PARRIS, LEON B PARRISH, LINDA C PARROTT, BETTY D   4._____

5. GROSS, ELANA
   A GROSS, ELAINE B GROSS, ELIZABETH C GROSS, ELLIOT D   5._____

6. HORSTMANN, ANNA
   A HORSMAN, ALLAN B HORST, VALERIE C HORSTMAN, JAMES D   6._____

7. JONES, EMILY
   A JONES, ELMA B JONES, ELOISE C JONES, EMMA D   7._____

8. LESSING, FRED
   A LESSER, MARTHA B LESSIN, ELLIE C LESSNER, ERWIN D   8._____

9. ROSENBLUM, JULIUS
   A ROSENBLUTH, SYLVIA B ROSENBORG, ERIC C ROSENBURG, JANE D   9._____

10. YOUNG, THEODORE
    A YOUNG, TERRY B YOUNG, THELMA C YOUNG, THOMAS D   10._____

11. RENICK, KAREN
    A RENIE, JOSEPH B RENITA, JOSE C RENKO, DORIS D   11._____

12. ADLER, HELEN
    A ADLER, HAROLD B ADLER, HARRY C ADLER, HENRY D   12._____

13. BURKHARDT, ANN
    A BURKET, HARRIET B BURKHOLDER, CARL C BURKHOLZ, SCOTT D   13._____

14. DE LUCA, PAUL
    A DE LUCA, JOHN B DE LUCIA, AUDREY C DE LUCIA, ROBERT D   14._____

15. DEMBSKI, STEPHEN
    A DEMBLING, JOAN B DEMBNER, PETER C DEMBROW, HELEN D   15._____

16. FLYNN, ARCHIE
    A FLYNN, AGNES B FLYNN, ANDREW C FLYNN, ANNMARIE D

    16.____

17. GRAFFY, PAUL
    A GRAFMAN, ANDREW B GRAFSTEIN, BETTY C GRAFTON, MELVIN D

    17.____

18. KERMIT, FRANK
    A KERMAN, LINDA B KERMISH, RHODA C KERMOYAN, MICKI D

    18.____

19. METZLER, MAURICE
    A METZGER, ALFRED B METZIER, SONIA C METZINGER, PAUL D

    19.____

20. PADDINGTON, TIMOTHY
    A PADDEN, MICHAEL B PADDISON, BRUCE C PADELL, EUNICE D

    20.____

21. RICHARDSON, BLANCHE
    A RICHARDSON, BETTY B RICHARDSON, BEVERLY C RICHARDSON, BRENDA D

    21.____

22. ISEKI, EMILE
    A ISELIN, CAROL B ISEN, RICHARD C ISENEE, CYNTHIA D

    22.____

23. CONNELL, EUGENE
    A CONNELL, EDWARD B CONNELL, HELEN C CONNELL, HUGH D

    23.____

24. MAC LEOD, LAURIE
    A MAC LEOD, LORNA B MC LANE, PAUL C MC LAREN, DUNCAN D

    24.____

25. BOLE, KENNETH
    A BOLDEN, ROSIE B BOLDT, LINDA C BOLELLA, DENNIS D

    25.____

KEY (CORRECT ANSWERS)

1.	B	11.	A
2.	D	12.	C
3.	B	13.	B
4.	C	14.	B
5.	B	15.	D
6.	D	16.	D
7.	C	17.	A
8.	C	18.	C
9.	A	19.	D
10.	C	20.	B

21. C
22. A
23. B
24. A
25. C

TEST 3

DIRECTIONS: For each of the following, you are given a name above and three other names in alphabetical order below. The letters A, B, C, and D stand for spaces where you could file the name. Find the CORRECT space for the name given above so that it will be in alphabetical order with the names below it. The letter that stands for that space is the answer to the question.

1. CARLISLE, ALAN 1._____
   A CARLINSKY, LEONA B CARLITOS, JUAN C CARLL, CHARLES D

2. COLLINS, KAREN 2._____
   A COLLINS, KATHLEEN B COLLINS, KATHRYN C COLLINS, KAY D

3. GALLOTTI, OSCAR 3._____
   A GALLONTY, FRANCIS B GALLOP, LILLIAN C GALLOU, ALEXIS D

4. MAHADY, JOHN 4._____
   A MAHADEO, PRATAB B MAHAJAN, ASHA C MAHARAJAH, MIARIAM D

5. WINGATE, REBECCA 5._____
   A WINGARD, LUCILLE B WINGAT, ROBERT C WINGER, HOLLY D

6. ZWEIGHAFT, FREDA 6._____
   A ZWEIG, BERTRAM B ZWEIGBAUM, BENJAMIN C ZWEIGENTHAL, DOROTHY D

7. MAXWELL, GEORGE 7._____
   A MAXWELL, EDWARD B MAXWELL, FRANK C MAXWELL, HARRIS D

8. O'DOHERTY, SALLY 8._____
   A ODETTE, CHARLES B ODIOTTI, MASSIE C ODNORALOV, MIKHAEL D

9. JAMES, ROGER 9._____
   A JAMIESON, KELLY B JAMNER, ELIZABETH C JAMPOLSKY, MILTON D

10. PADIN, FRANCIS 10._____
    A PADILLA, ANGELA B PADINGER, JENNY C PADLEY, RAYMOND D

11. AAARMAN, ALEC 11._____
    A AABY, JANE B AACH, ALBERT C AACHEN, HENRY D

12. BILLHARDT, PHILIP 12._____
    A BILLERA, FRANKLIN B BILLIG, LESLIE C BILLINGS, CAROL D

13. LADEROS, ELANA 13._____
    A LADENHEIM, HELENE B LADERMAN, SAM C LADHA, SANDRA D

14. PUCKERING, DENNIS 14._____
    A PUCKETT, AUDREY B PUCKNAT, JOHN C PUCKO, BENNY D

15. SCHOLZE, GEORGE 15._____
    A SCHOLNICK, LEONARD B SCHOLOSS, JACK C SCHOLZ, PAUL D

16. WILSON, MERYL
    A WILSON, MERIMAN B WILSON, MERRY C WILSON, MERRYL D

16.____

17. ZUKOWSKI, MICHAEL
    A ZWACK, ALEXA B ZYKO, KATHERINE C ZYMAN, HERBERT D

17.____

18. MC CANNA, THOMAS
    A MC CANN, GERALD B MC CANNA, JANET C MC CANTS, MOLLIE D

18.____

19. PHILIPP, SUSANE
    A PHILIP, PETER B PHILIPOSE, ANDREW C PHILIPPE, BEATRICE D

19.____

20. KINGPIN, PAUL
    A KINGDON, KENNETH B KINGMAN, JEAN C KINGOLD, RICHARD D

20.____

21. HAMILTON, DONALD
    A HAMILTON, DON B HAMILTON, DOROTHY C HAMILTON, DOUGLAS D

21.____

22. BAEL, ELAINE
    A BAELE, GUSTAVE B BAEN, JAMES C BAENA, ARIEL D

22.____

23. BILL, KASEY
    A BILGINER, NATHAN B BILKAY, WILLIAM C BILLES, BRADFORD D

23.____

24. CARLEN, ELLIOT
    A CARINO, NAN B CARLE, JOHN C CARLESI, ANTHONY D

24.____

25. LOURIE, DONALD
    A LOUIE, ROSE B LOUIS, STEVE C LOVE, MARCIA D

25.____

KEY (CORRECT ANSWERS)

1.	B	11.	A
2.	A	12.	B
3.	C	13.	C
4.	B	14.	A
5.	C	15.	D
6.	D	16.	D
7.	C	17.	A
8.	D	18.	C
9.	A	19.	C
10.	B	20.	D

21. B
22. A
23. C
24. C
25. C

TEST 4

DIRECTIONS: For each of the following, you are given a name above and three other names in alphabetical order below. The letters A, B, C, and D stand for spaces where you could file the name. Find the CORRECT space for the name given above so that it will be in alphabetical order with the names below it. The letter that stands for that space is the answer to the question.

1. DEMOPOULOS, GUS
   A DEMOPOULOS, DIMITRI B DEMOPOULOS, HELEN C DEMOPOULOS, LAURA D

   1.____

2. DRUMWRIGHT, BRUCE
   A DRUMMOND, RANDY B DRUMMUND, WALTER C DRUMRIGHT, JULIUS D

   2.____

3. GRAHAM, LETICIA
   A GRAHAM, LEON B GRAHAM, LEROY C GRAHAM, LESLIE D

   3.____

4. KELLEHER, KEVIN
   A KELLARD, WILLIAM B KELLEDY, JAMES C KELLEHER, KRISTINE D

   4.____

5. LIANG, JAN
   A LIANG, JIE B LIANG, JIN CHANG C LIANG, JIN HE D

   5.____

6. MOLINELLI, STEVE
   A MOLINAR, RICARDO B MOLINER, LOUISA C MOLINI, OSCAR D

   6.____

7. PARRILLA, EMANUEL
   A PARRAS, TONY B PARRETTA, JOSEPHINE C PARRETTA, NANCY D

   7.____

8. SILBERFARD, MILDRED
   A SILBERBERG, SEYMOUR B SILBERBLATT, JOHN C SILBERFARB, SYLVIA D

   8.____

9. TOLANI, ROHET
   A TOLAN, DOROTHY B TOLASSI, JOANNA C TOLBERT, ALICE D

   9.____

10. VIERA, DIANE
    A VIERA, DIANA B VIERA, ELLIOT C VIERA, JAMES D

    10.____

11. KLAUER, MICHAEL
    A KLAUBER, ALFRED B KLAUBERG, SUSAN C KLAUS, MARJORIE D

    11.____

12. REEVES, MARIE
    A REEVES, MATTHEW B REEVES, MELVIN C REEVES, ORALEE D

    12.____

13. DEL VALLE, JULIA
    A DEL VALLE, EMMA B DEL VALLE, GLORIA C DEL VALLE, JOSEPH D

    13.____

14. LAIO, SHU-YU
    A LAING, VINCENT B LAIRO, SCOTT C LAIS, STEVE D

    14.____

15. MENDEZ, ROBERTO
    A MENDELSON, SOL B MENDES, MAE C MENDOZA, HUGO D

    15.____

16. ALBRIGHT, LEE 16.____
    A ALBRACHT, MARIE B ALBRECHT, VICTOR C ALBRINK, JOAN D

17. CAIN, STEPHEN 17.____
    A CAIN, SAMUEL B CAIN, SHARON C CAIN, SIBOL D

18. HOPKOWITZ, THOMAS 18.____
    A HOPKINS, CYNTHIA B HOPPENFELD, DENIS C HOPPER, ELSA D

19. LUMBLY, KAREN 19.____
    A LUMBI, JENNY B LUME, JIMMIE C LUMEN, GAIL D

20. MAYER, MORTON 20.____
    A MAYER, MONROE B MAYER, MORRIS C MAYER, MYRON D

21. YOUNGER, LORRAINE 21.____
    A YOUNGHEM, THEODORE B YOUNGMAN, LEIF C YOUNGS, FRED D

22. THORSEN, HILDA 22.____
    A THORNWELL, PERCY B THORON, LLOYD C THORP, JACQUELINE D

23. MC DERMOTT, BETTY 23.____
    A MC DEARMON, WILLIAM B MC DEVITT, BERYL C MC DONAGH, DANIEL D

24. BLUMENTHAL, SIMON 24.____
    A BLUMENTHAL, SHIRLEY B BLUMENTHAL, SIDNEY C BLUMENTHAL, SOLOMON D

25. ERVINS, RICHARD 25.____
    A ERVIN, BERTHA B ERVING, THELMA C ERWIN, EUGENE D

KEY (CORRECT ANSWERS)

1.	B	11.	C
2.	D	12.	A
3.	D	13.	D
4.	C	14.	B
5.	A	15.	C
6.	B	16.	C
7.	D	17.	D
8.	D	18.	B
9.	B	19.	B
10.	B	20.	C

21. A
22. D
23. B
24. C
25. C

TEST 5

DIRECTIONS: For each of the following, you are given a name above and three other names in alphabetical order below. The letters A, B, C, and D stand for spaces where you could file the name. Find the CORRECT space for the name given above so that it will be in alphabetical order with the names below it. The letter that stands for that space is the answer to the question.

1. GUIDRY, THELMA
   A GUIDONE, GEORGE B GUIGLI, PAMELA C GUIGNON, DANIEL D

2. JAMES, ALLAN
   A JAMES, ALMA B JAMES, AMY C JAMES, ANNA D

3. LESSOFF, CONNIE
   A LESSIK, JAKE B LESSING, LEONARD C LESSNER, ADELE D

4. MONTNER, LUIS
   A MONTEFIORE, ANDREW B MONTILLA, IRIS C MONTINI, ALEXANDRA D

5. PHELPS, KENNETH
   A PHELEN, JAMES B PHELON, RANDY C PHETT, GARY D

6. STAVSKY, STANLEY
   A STAVROS, MIKE B STAWSKI, LILLIAN C STAWSKI, NAOMI D

7. GROSSMAN, WILL
   A GROSSMAN, WENDY B GROSSMANN, WAYNE C GROSSMANN, WILLA D

8. IRES, JEFFREY
   A IRENA, THOMAS B IRENE, JAY C IRES, HOWARD D

9. NIKOLAOU, CHRISTINE
   A NIKOLAIS, GERRARD B NIKOLAKAKOS, GEORGE C NIKOLATOS, HARRY D

10. TURCO, KEITH
    A TURCHIN, DEBORAH B TURCI, GINA C TURCK, KATHRYN D

11. WORLEY, DIANE
    A WORMAN, STELLA B WORMER, SARA C WORMLEY, ROBERT D

12. DRUSIN, GUY
    A DRURY, JESSICA B DRUSE, KEN C DRUSS, THERESA D

13. LYONS, JAMES
    A LYONS, ERNST B LYONS, INGRID C LYONS, KEVIN D

14. NOBLE, BERNARD
    A NOBEL, LOUISE B NOBILE, DENNIS C NOBIS, JAMES D

15. O'DELL, ERIN
    A O'DAY, PATRICIA B O'DEA, MAUREEN C O'DELL, GWYNN D

16. POUPON, LOUIS
    A POULSON, SIMON B POURE, DAMIAN C POURIDAS, CARMEN D

16. ____

17. REMEY, NAOMI
    A REMES, STUART B REMEZ, ALFREDO C REMIEN, ROBERT D

17. ____

18. WATSON, LAURENCE
    A WATSON, LENORA B WATSON, LEONARD C WATSON, LLOYD D

18. ____

19. AMSILI, MORTON
    A AMSDEN, ESTHER B AMSEL, HYMAN C ARES, MEYER D

19. ____

20. CLEMMONS, BERTHA
    A CLEMENT, GILBERT B CLEMINSON, DEAN C CLEMONS, GLADYS D

20. ____

21. LAMPERT, EDNA
    A LAMPIER, JANICE B LAMPKIN, ALYCE C LAMPKOWSKI, DENNIS D

21. ____

22. LIBERTO, DON
    A LIBERMAN, MATTIE B LIBERSON, MIRIAM C LIBERTY, ARTHUR D

22. ____

23. REVENZON, ISABELLA
    A REVELEY, RUTH B REVELLE, GRACE C REVERE, EDITH D

23. ____

24. BURKHALTER, HAZEL
    A BURKE, WINSTON B BURKETT, BENJAMIN C BURKEY, WAYNE D

24. ____

25. DORSEY, HAROLD
    A DOSHER, EILEEN B DOSHIRE, BURTON C DOSSIL, RICHARD D

25. ____

KEY (CORRECT ANSWERS)

1.	B	11.	A
2.	A	12.	C
3.	D	13.	C
4.	D	14.	D
5.	C	15.	C
6.	B	16.	B
7.	B	17.	B
8.	D	18.	A
9.	C	19.	C
10.	D	20.	C

21. A
22. C
23. C
24. D
25. A

TEST 6

DIRECTIONS: For each of the following, you are given a name above and three other names in alphabetical order below. The letters A, B, C, and D stand for spaces where you could file the name. Find the CORRECT space for the name given above so that it will be in alphabetical order with the names below it. The letter that stands for that space is the answer to the question.

1. HATFIELD, NICOLA
   A HATCHER, JOHN B HATELY, BRIAN C HATGIS, ELLEN D

2. IVANOFF, HELENA
   A IVAN, LEONARD B IVANOV, SERGE C IVANY, EMERY D

3. KELKER, NORMAN
   A KELFER, STEPHANE B KELING, JAY C KELISON, ABE D

4. ROGGENBURG, LEE
   A ROGERS, SHARON B ROGET, ALLAN C ROGGERO, MORGAN D

5. SMITH, ALENA
   A SMITH, AARON B SMITH, AGNES C SMITH, ALBERT D

6. ZOLOR, RONALD
   A ZOLNAK, SUSANNA B ZOLOTH, SAMUEL C ZOLOTO, PEARL D

7. ERRICH, GRETCHEN
   A ERREICH, RENE B ERRERA, STEVEN C ERRETT, ALICE D

8. CARDWELL, MELASAN
   A CARDUCCI, RONALD B CARDULLO, MIKE C CARDY, FREDRIK D

9. MOFFAT, SARAH
   A MOFFET, JONATHAN B MOFFIE, LISA C MOFFITT, LAUREN D

10. PARRINO, WAYNE
    A PARRETTA, MICHELE B PARRILLA, BERNIE C PARRINELLO, CARRIE D

11. PINSLEY, SETH
    A PINSKY, GLORIA B PINSON, BENNET C PINTADO, MARIE D

12. FREEMAN, ELMIRA
    A FREEMAN, EDITH B FREEMAN, ERIC C FREEMAN, ETHEL D

13. BERLINGER, SOPHIE
    A BERLEY, DAVID B BERLIND, ARNOLD C BERLINGER, FREDA D

14. ANIELLO, JOSEPH
    A ANGULO, ADOLFO B ANHALT, LINDA C ANIBAL, VINCENT D

15. LACHER, LEO
    A LACHET, MARGARET B LACHINI, KAY C LACHIVER, ANDREA D

16. ROBINSON, MARION 16.___
    A ROBINSON, MARCIA B ROBINSON, MARGARET C ROBINSON, MARIETTA D

17. ULRICH, DENNIS 17.___
    A ULMAN, CANDY B ULMER, TED C ULRIED, RICHARD D

18. ASHINSKY, ROSS 18.___
    A ASHKAR, MICHAEL B ASHKE, PAUL C ASHKIN, ROBERTA D

19. LITVAK, DARRELL 19.___
    A LITUCHY, BEVERLY B LITVIN, SAM C LITWACK, MARTIN D

20. SLATTERY, GERALD 20.___
    A SLATER, NELLIE B SLATKIN, HEIDI C SLATKY, IRVING D

21. MCCANTS, GEORGIA 21.___
    A MCCANN, CHERYL B MCCANNA, THOMAS C MCCARDELL, GARY D

22. HARMER, AVA 22.___
    A HARLOW, JULES B HARLSON, NORMAN C HARMEL, SHARON D

23. CALDERONE, PHILIP 23.___
    A CALDERIN, ANA B CALDON, WALTER C CALDRON, MICHELE D

24. GINSBURG, ISAAC 24.___
    A GINSBURG, EDWARD B GINSBURG, GERALD C GINSBURG, HILDA D

25. LEE, LEIGH 25.___
    A LEE, LELA B LEE, LELAND C LEE, LEON D

KEY (CORRECT ANSWERS)

1.	C	11.	B
2.	B	12.	B
3.	D	13.	D
4.	C	14.	D
5.	D	15.	A
6.	B	16.	D
7.	D	17.	C
8.	C	18.	A
9.	A	19.	B
10.	D	20.	D

21. C
22. D
23. B
24. D
25. A

TEST 7

DIRECTIONS: For each of the following, you are given a name above and three other names in alphabetical order below. The letters A, B, C, and D stand for spaces where you could file the name. Find the CORRECT space for the name given above so that it will be in alphabetical order with the names below it. The letter that stands for that space is the answer to the question.

1. POWERS, PHYLLIS
   A POWELL, HATTIE B POWER, EDWARD C POWLETT, WENDY D

   1.____

2. SILVERA, IRWIN
   A SILVA, ANGEL B SILVANO, FRANK C SILVERIA, ANNA D

   2.____

3. BACHRACH, DAN
   A BACHMANN, DONNA B BACHNER, LESTER C BACHOWSKI, JEWEL D

   3.____

4. RIVERA, RAMON
   A RIVAS, ERICA B RIVES, SHARON C RIVIER, CLAUDE D

   4.____

5. WEINSTOCK, JEFFREY
   A WEINSTEIN, PAUL B WEINSTONE, ALAN C WEINTRAUB, MARCI D

   5.____

6. AMANDA, STEPHAN
   A AMADO, DANIELLO B AMALIA, JOSE C AMAR, LISA D

   6.____

7. HERRON, LOUIS
   A HERSCH, JACK B HERSCHELL, GREGORY C HERSCHER, GAIL D

   7.____

8. REEDY, ARTHUR
   A REED, ALEX B REESE, JOHN C REEVE, DAVE D

   8.____

9. FLORIN, RAYMOND
   A FLORENTINO, PAULA B FLORES, MITCHEL C FLORIAN, CARLO D

   9.____

10. HOROWITZ, ELLIOT
    A HOROWITZ, FRANKLIN B HOROWITZ, IRA C HOROWITZ, JOAN D

    10.____

11. KNOPFLER, WOODY
    A KNOBLER, HENRY B KNOLL, GEORGE C KNOPF, LAURA D

    11.____

12. OTIN, JENNIFER
    A OTERO, ALBERT B OTHON, DOROTHY C OTIS, JAMES D

    12.____

13. SACHA, IRENE
    A SACCO, HEATHER B SACHNER, JULIE C SACHS, DAVID D

    13.____

14. WORTHY, PRISCILLA
    A WORTH, ROBERT B WORTHINGTON, SUSAN C WORTMAN, MYRA D

    14.____

15. ZUCKERMAN, GARY
    A ZUKER, JEROME B ZUKOWSKI, CHRIS C ZULACK, JOHN D

    15.____

2 (#7)

16. BRIEGER, CLARENCE
    A BRIEF, SIGMUND B BRIELLE, JEAN C BRIELOFF, SAUL D

    16.____

17. FOSTER, AGNES
    A FOSTER, ADDIE B FOSTER, ALBERT C FOSTER, ALICE D

    17.____

18. LIBERSTEIN, MIRIAM
    A LIBERMAN, HERMAN B LIBERSON, RUBIN C LIBERT, NAT D

    18.____

19. PRICKETT, DELORES
    A PRICE, WILLIAM B PRICHARD, STEPHANY C PRITCHETT, KENNETH D

    19.____

20. TRIBBLE, RITA
    A TRIAS, JOSE B TRIBBIT, CHARLES C TRIBE, SIENNA D

    20.____

21. ZOBEL, MAX
    A ZOBACK, DERRICK B ZOBALI, KIERSTAN C ZOBERG, STUART D

    21.____

22. HOTRA, WALTER
    A HOTT, NELL B HOTTENSEN, ROBERT C HOTON, BRUCE D

    22.____

23. MICHELL, CARL
    A MICHELE, KAREN B MICHELMAN, BERTHA C MICHELS, GLORIA D

    23.____

24. RAFFERTY, GEORGE
    A RAFFERTY, HAROLD B RAFFERTY, KEVIN C RAFFERTY, LUCILLE D

    24.____

25. OLIVIERI, ALLAN
    A OLIVIERO, FRANK B OLIVRY, RAUL C OLIZEIRA, CHARLES D

    25.____

KEY (CORRECT ANSWERS)

1.	C	11.	D
2.	C	12.	C
3.	D	13.	B
4.	B	14.	C
5.	B	15.	A
6.	C	16.	B
7.	A	17.	B
8.	B	18.	C
9.	D	19.	C
10.	A	20.	C

21. C
22. A
23. B
24. A
25. A

RECORD KEEPING
EXAMINATION SECTION
TEST 1

DIRECTIONS: Each question or incomplete statement is followed by several suggested answers or completions. Select the one that BEST answers the question or completes the statement. *PRINT THE LETTER OF THE CORRECT ANSWER IN THE SPACE AT THE RIGHT.*

Questions 1-7.

DIRECTIONS: In answering Questions 1 through 7, use the following master list. For each question, determine where the name would fit on the master list. Each answer choice indicates right before or after the name in the answer choice.

    Aaron, Jane
    Armstead, Brendan
    Bailey, Charles
    Dent, Ricardo
    Grant, Mark
    Mars, Justin
    Methieu, Justine
    Parker, Cathy
    Sampson, Suzy
    Thomas, Heather

1. Schmidt, William
    A. Right before Cathy Parker
    B. Right after Heather Thomas
    C. Right after Suzy Sampson
    D. Right before Ricardo Dent

2. Asanti, Kendall
    A. Right before Jane Aaron
    B. Right after Charles Bailey
    C. Right before Justine Methieu
    D. Right after Brendan Armstead

3. O'Brien, Daniel
    A. Right after Justine Methieu
    B. Right before Jane Aaron
    C. Right after Mark Grant
    D. Right before Suzy Sampson

4. Marrow, Alison
    A. Right before Cathy Parker
    B. Right before Justin Mars
    C. Right before Mark Grant
    D. Right after Heather Thomas

5. Grantt, Marissa
    A. Right before Mark Grant
    B. Right after Mark Grant
    C. Right after Justin Mars
    D. Right before Suzy Sampson

1.____
2.____
3.____
4.____
5.____

2 (#1)

6. Thompson, Heath   6.____
   A. Right after Justin Mars   B. Right before Suzy Sampson
   C. Right after Heather Thomas   D. Right before Cathy Parker

DIRECTIONS: Before answering Question 7, add in all of the names from Questions 1 through 6. Then fit the name in alphabetical order based on the new list.

7. Francisco, Mildred   7.____
   A. Right before Mark Grant   B. Right after Marissa Grantt
   C. Right before Alison Marrow   D. Right after Kendall Asanti

Questions 8-10.

DIRECTIONS: In answering Questions 8 through 10, compare each pair of names and addresses. Indicate whether they are the same or different in any way.

8. William H. Pratt, J.D.   William H. Pratt, J.D.   8.____
   Attourney at Law   Attorney at Law
   A. No differences   B. 1 difference
   C. 2 differences   D. 3 differences

9. 1303 Theater Drive,; Apt. 3-B   1330 Theatre Drive,; Apt. 3-B   9.____
   A. No differences   B. 1 difference
   C. 2 differences   D. 3 differences

10. Petersdorff, Briana and Mary   Petersdorff, Briana and Mary   10.____
    A. No differences   B. 1 difference
    C. 2 differences   D. 3 differences

11. Which of the following words, if any, are misspelled?   11.____
    A. Affordable   B. Circumstansial
    C. Legalese   D. None of the above

Questions 12-13.

DIRECTIONS: Questions 12 and 13 are to be answered on the basis of the following table.

Standardized Test Results for High School Students in District #1230

	English	Math	Science	Reading
High School 1	21	22	15	18
High School 2	12	16	13	15
High School 3	16	18	21	17
High School 4	19	14	15	16

The scores for each high school in the district were averaged out and listed for each subject tested. Scores of 0-10 are significantly below College Readiness Standards. 11-15 are below College Readiness, 16-20 meet College Readiness, and 21-25 are above College Readiness.

12. If the high schools need to meet or exceed in at least half the categories in order to NOT be considered "at risk," which schools are considered "at risk"?   12.____
    A. High School 2   B. High School 3
    C. High School 4   D. Both A and C

13. What percentage of subjects did the district as a whole meet or exceed College Readiness standards?   13.____
    A. 25%   B. 50%   C. 75%   D. 100%

Questions 14-15.

DIRECTIONS: Questions 14 and 15 are to be answered on the basis of the following information.

You have seven employees working as a part of your team: Austin, Emily, Jeremy, Christina, Martin, Harriet, and Steve. You have just sent an e-mail informing them that there will be a mandatory training session next week. To ensure that work still gets done, you are offering the training twice during the week: once on Tuesday and also on Thursday. This way half the employees will still be working while the other half attend the training. The only other issue is that Jeremy doesn't work on Tuesdays and Harriet doesn't work on Thursdays due to compressed work schedules.

14. Which of the following is a possible attendance roster for the first training session?   14.____
    A. Emily, Jeremy, Steve   B. Steve, Christina, Harriet
    C. Harriet, Jeremy, Austin   D. Steve, Martin, Jeremy

15. If Harriet, Christina, and Steve attend the training session on Tuesday, which of the following is a possible roster for Thursday's training session?   15.____
    A. Jeremy, Emily, and Austin   B. Emily, Martin, and Harriet
    C. Austin, Christina, and Emily D. Jeremy, Emily, and Steve

Questions 16-20.

DIRECTIONS: In answering Questions 16 through 20, you will be given a word and will need to choose the answer choice that is MOST similar or different to the word.

16. Which word means the SAME as *annual*?   16.____
    A. Monthly   B. Usually   C. Yearly   D. Constantly

17. Which word means the SAME as *effort*?   17.____
    A. Energy   B. Equate   C. Cherish   D. Commence

18. Which word means the OPPOSITE of *forlorn*?   18.____
    A. Neglected   B. Lethargy   C. Optimistic   D. Astonished

19. Which word means the SAME as *risk*?   19.____
    A. Admire   B. Hazard   C. Limit   D. Hesitant

20. Which word means the OPPOSITE of *translucent*?
    A. Opaque   B. Transparent   C. Luminous   D. Introverted

21. Last year, Jamie's annual salary was $50,000. Her boss called her today to inform her that she would receive a 20% raise for the upcoming year. How much more money will Jamie receive next year?
    A. $60,000   B. $10,000   C. $1,000   D. $51,000

22. You and a co-worker work for a temp hiring agency as part of their office staff. You both are given 6 days off per month. How many days off are you and your co-worker given in a year?
    A. 24   B. 72   C. 144   D. 48

23. If Margot makes $34,000 per year and she works 40 hours per week for all 52 weeks, what is her hourly rate?
    A. $16.34/hour   B. $17.00/hour   C. $15.54/hour   D. $13.23/hour

24. How many dimes are there in $175.00?
    A. 175   B. 1,750   C. 3,500   D. 17,500

25. If Janey is three times as old as Emily, and Emily is 3, how old is Janey?
    A. 6   B. 9   C. 12   D. 15

KEY (CORRECT ANSWERS)

1.	C		11.	B
2.	D		12.	A
3.	A		13.	D
4.	B		14.	B
5.	B		15.	A
6.	C		16.	C
7.	A		17.	A
8.	B		18.	C
9.	C		19.	B
10.	A		20.	A

21. B
22. C
23. A
24. B
25. B

TEST 2

DIRECTIONS: Each question or incomplete statement is followed by several suggested answers or completions. Select the one that BEST answers the question or completes the statement. *PRINT THE LETTER OF THE CORRECT ANSWER IN THE SPACE AT THE RIGHT.*

Questions 1-6.

DIRECTIONS: Questions 1 through 6 are to be answered on the basis of the following information.

item	name of item to be ordered
quantity	minimum number that can be ordered
beginning amount	amount in stock at start of month
amount received	amount receiving during month
ending amount	amount in stock at end of month
amount used	amount used during month
amount to order	will need at least as much of each item as used in the previous month
unit price	cost of each unit of an item
total price	total price for the order

Item	Quantity	Beginning	Received	Ending	Amount Used	Amount to Order	Unit Price	Total Price
Pens	10	22	10	8	24	20	$0.11	$2.20
Spiral notebooks	8	30	13	12			$0.25	
Binder clips	2 boxes	3 boxes	1 box	1 box			$1.79	
Sticky notes	3 packs	12 packs	4 packs	2 packs			$1.29	
Dry erase markers	1 pack (dozen)	34 markers	8 markers	10 markers			$16.49	
Ink cartridges (printer)	1 cartridge	3 cartridges	1 cartridge	2 cartridges			$79.99	
Folders	10 folders	25 folders	15 folders	10 folders			$1.08	

1. How many packs of sticky notes were used during the month?
    A. 16   B. 10   C. 12   D. 14

2. How many folders need to be ordered for next month?
    A. 15   B. 20   C. 30   D. 40

3. What is the total price of notebooks that you will need to order?
    A. $6.00   B. $0.25   C. $4.50   D. $2.75

4. Which of the following will you spend the second most money on?
    A. Ink cartridges   B. Dry erase markers
    C. Sticky notes   D. Binder clips

5. How many packs of dry erase markers should you order?
    A. 1   B. 8   C. 12   D. 0

6. What will be the total price of the file folders you order? 6.____
   A. $20.16   B. $21.60   C. $10.80   D. $4.32

Questions 7-11.

DIRECTIONS: Questions 7 through 11 are to be answered on the basis of the following table.

Number of Car Accidents, By Location and Cause, for 2014						
	Location 1		Location 2		Location 3	
Cause	Number	Percent	Number	Percent	Number	Percent
Severe Weather	10		25		30	
Excessive Speeding	20	40	5		10	
Impaired Driving	15		15	25	8	
Miscellaneous	5		15		2	4
TOTALS	50	100	60	100	50	100

7. Which of the following is the third highest cause of accidents for all three locations? 7.____
   A. Severe Weather   B. Impaired Driving
   C. Miscellaneous   D. Excessive Speeding

8. The average number of Severe Weather accidents per week at Location 3 for the year (52 weeks) was MOST NEARLY 8.____
   A. 0.57   B. 30   C. 1   D. 1.25

9. Which location had the LARGEST percentage of accidents caused by Impaired Driving? 9.____
   A. 1   B. 2   C. 3   D. Both A and B

10. If one-third of the accidents at all three locations resulted in at least one fatality, what is the LEAST amount of deaths caused by accidents last year? 10.____
    A. 60   B. 106   C. 66   D. 53

11. What is the percentage of accidents caused by miscellaneous means from all three locations in 2014? 11.____
    A. 5%   B. 10%   C. 13%   D. 25%

12. How many pairs of the following groups of letters are exactly alike? 12.____
    ACDOBJ   ACDBOJ
    HEWBWR   HEWRWB
    DEERVS   DEERVS
    BRFQSX   BRFQSX
    WEYRVB   WEYRVB
    SPQRZA   SQRPZA

    A. 2   B. 3   C. 4   D. 5

Questions 13-19.

DIRECTIONS: Questions 13 through 19 are to be answered on the basis of the following information.

In 2012, the most current information on the American population was finished. The information was compiled by 200 volunteers in each of the 50 states. The territory of Puerto Rico, a sovereign of the United States, had 25 people assigned to compile data. In February of 2010, volunteers in each state and sovereign began collecting information. In Puerto Rico, data collection finished by January 31st, 2011, while work in the United States was completed on June 30, 2012. Each volunteer gathered data on the population of their state or sovereign. When the information was compiled, volunteers sent reports to the nation's capital, Washington, D.C. Each volunteer worked 20 hours per month and put together 10 reports per month. After the data was compiled in total, 50 people reviewed the data and worked from January 2012 to December 2012.

13. How many reports were generated from February 2010 to April 2010 in Illinois and Ohio?
    A. 3,000 B. 6,000 C. 12,000 D. 15,000
    13.____

14. How many volunteers in total collected population data in January 2012?
    A. 10,000 B. 2,000 C. 225 D. 200
    14.____

15. How many reports were put together in May 2012?
    A. 2,000 B. 50,000 C. 100,000 D. 100,250
    15.____

16. How many hours did the Puerto Rican volunteers work in the fall (September-November)?
    A. 60 B. 500 C. 1,500 D. 0
    16.____

17. How many workers were compiling or reviewing data in July 2012?
    A. 25 B. 50 C. 200 D. 250
    17.____

18. What was the total amount of hours worked by Nevada volunteers in July 2010?
    A. 500 B. 4,000 C. 4,500 D. 5,000
    18.____

19. How many reviewers worked in January 2013?
    A. 75 B. 50 C. 0 D. 25
    19.____

20. John has to file 10 documents per shelf. How many documents would it take for John to fill 40 shelves?
    A. 40 B. 400 C. 4,500 D. 5,000
    20.____

21. Jill wants to travel from New York City to Los Angeles by bike, which is approximately 2,772 miles. How many miles per day would Jill need to average if she wanted to complete the trip in 4 weeks?
    A. 100 B. 89 C. 99 D. 94
    21.____

22. If there are 24 CPU's and only 7 monitors, how many more monitors do you need to have the same amount of monitors as CPU's?
    A. Not enough information
    B. 17
    C. 31
    D. 0

23. If Gerry works 5 days a week and 8 hours each day, and John works 3 days a week and 10 hours each day, how many more hours per year will Gerry work than John?
    A. They work the same amount of hours.
    B. 450
    C. 520
    D. 832

24. Jimmy gets transferred to a new office. The new office has 25 employees, but only 16 are there due to a blizzard. How many coworkers was Jimmy able to meet on his first day?
    A. 16
    B. 25
    C. 9
    D. 7

25. If you do a fundraiser for charities in your area and raise $500 total, how much would you give to each charity if you were donating equal amounts to 3 of them?
    A. $250.00
    B. $167.77
    C. $50.00
    D. $111.11

KEY (CORRECT ANSWERS)

1.	D	11.	C
2.	B	12.	B
3.	A	13.	C
4.	C	14.	A
5.	D	15.	C
6.	B	16.	C
7.	D	17.	B
8.	A	18.	B
9.	A	19.	C
10.	D	20.	B

21.	C
22.	B
23.	C
24.	A
25.	B

TEST 3

DIRECTIONS: Each question or incomplete statement is followed by several suggested answers or completions. Select the one that BEST answers the question or completes the statement. *PRINT THE LETTER OF THE CORRECT ANSWER IN THE SPACE AT THE RIGHT.*

Questions 1-3.

DIRECTIONS: In answering Questions 1 through 3, choose the correctly spelled word.

1. A. allusion B. alusion C. allusien D. allution 1.____
2. A. altitude B. alltitude C. atlitude D. altlitude 2.____
3. A. althogh B. allthough C. althrough D. although 3.____

Questions 4-9.

DIRECTIONS: In answering Questions 4 through 9, choose the answer that BEST completes the analogy.

4. Odometer is to mileage as compass is to 4.____
   A. speed B. needle C. hiking D. direction

5. Marathon is to race as hibernation is to 5.____
   A. winter B. dream C. sleep D. bear

6. Cup is to coffee as bowl is to 6.____
   A. dish B. spoon C. food D. soup

7. Flow is to river as stagnant is to 7.____
   A. pool B. rain C. stream D. canal

8. Paw is to cat as hoof is to 8.____
   A. lamb B. horse C. lion D. elephant

9. Architect is to building as sculptor is to 9.____
   A. museum B. chisel C. stone D. statue

Questions 10-14.

DIRECTIONS: Questions 10 through 14 are to be answered on the basis of the following graph.

Population of Carroll City Broken Down by Age and Gender (in Thousands)			
Age	Female	Male	Total
Under 15	60	60	120
15-23		22	
24-33		20	44
34-43	13	18	31
44-53	20		67
64 and Over	65	65	130
TOTAL	230	232	462

10. How many people in the city are between the ages of 15-23?
    A. 70   B. 46,000   C. 70,000   D. 225,000

11. Approximately what percentage of the total population of the city was female aged 24-33?
    A. 10%   B. 5%   C. 15%   D. 25%

12. If 33% of the males have a job and 55% of females don't have a job, which of the following statements is TRUE?
    A. Males have approximately 2,600 more jobs than females.
    B. Females have approximately 49,000 more jobs than males.
    C. Females have approximately 26,000 more jobs than males.
    D. None of the above statements are true.

13. How many females between the ages of 15-23 live in Carroll City?
    A. 67,000   B. 24,000   C. 48,000   D. 91,000

14. Assume all males 44-53 living in Carroll City are employed. If two-thirds of males age 44-53 work jobs outside of Carroll City, how many work within city limits?
    A. 31,333
    B. 15,667
    C. 47,000
    D. Cannot answer the question with the information provided

Questions 15-16.

DIRECTIONS: Questions 15 and 16 are labeled as shown. Alphabetize them for filing. Choose the answer that correctly shows the order.

15. (1) AED
    (2) OOS
    (3) FOA
    (4) DOM
    (5) COB

    A. 2-5-4-3-2   B. 1-4-5-2-3   C. 1-5-4-2-3   D. 1-5-4-3-2

15.____

16. Alphabetize the names of the people. Last names are given last.
    (1) Lindsey Jamestown
    (2) Jane Alberta
    (3) Ally Jamestown
    (4) Allison Johnston
    (5) Lyle Moreno

    A. 2-1-3-4-5   B. 3-4-2-1-5   C. 2-3-1-4-5   D. 4-3-2-1-5

16.____

17. Which of the following words is misspelled?
    A. disgust
    B. whisper
    C. locale
    D. none of the above

17.____

Questions 18-21.

DIRECTIONS: Questions 18 through 21 are to be answered on the basis of the following list of employees.

Robertson, Aaron
Bacon, Gina
Jerimiah, Trace
Gillette, Stanley
Jacks, Sharon

18. Which employee name would come in third in alphabetized list?
    A. Robertson, Aaron
    B. Jerimiah, Trace
    C. Gillette, Stanley
    D. Jacks, Sharon

18.____

19. Which employee's first name starts with the letter in the alphabet that is five letters after the first letter of their last name?
    A. Jerimiah, Trace
    B. Bacon, Gina
    C. Jacks, Sharon
    D. Gillette, Stanley

19.____

20. How many employees have last names that are exactly five letters long?
    A. 1   B. 2   C. 3   D. 4

20.____

21. How many of the employees have either a first or last name that starts with the letter "G"? 21.____
    A. 1   B. 2   C. 4   D. 5

Questions 22-25.

DIRECTIONS: Questions 22 through 25 are to be answered on the basis of the following chart.

Bicycle Sales (Model #34JA32)							
Country	May	June	July	August	September	October	Total
Germany	34	47	45	54	56	60	296
Britain	40	44	36	47	47	46	260
Ireland	37	32	32	32	34	33	200
Portugal	14	14	14	16	17	14	89
Italy	29	29	28	31	29	31	177
Belgium	22	24	24	26	25	23	144
Total	176	198	179	206	208	207	1166

22. What percentage of the overall total was sold to the German importer? 22.____
    A. 25.3%   B. 22%   C. 24.1%   D. 23%

23. What percentage of the overall total was sold in September? 23.____
    A. 24.1%   B. 25.6%   C. 17.9%   D. 24.6%

24. What is the average number of units per month imported into Belgium over the first four months shown? 24.____
    A. 26   B. 20   C. 24   D. 31

25. If you look at the three smallest importers, what is their total import percentage? 25.____
    A. 35.1%   B. 37.1%   C. 40%   D. 28%

KEY (CORRECT ANSWERS)

1.	A	11.	B
2.	A	12.	C
3.	D	13.	C
4.	D	14.	B
5.	C	15.	D
6.	D	16.	C
7.	A	17.	D
8.	B	18.	D
9.	D	19.	B
10.	C	20.	B

21. B
22. A
23. C
24. C
25. A

TEST 4

DIRECTIONS: Each question or incomplete statement is followed by several suggested answers or completions. Select the one that BEST answers the question or completes the statement. *PRINT THE LETTER OF THE CORRECT ANSWER IN THE SPACE AT THE RIGHT.*

Questions 1-6.

DIRECTIONS: In answering Questions 1 through 6, choose the sentence that represents the BEST example of English grammar.

1. A. Joey and me want to go on a vacation next week.
   B. Gary told Jim he would need to take some time off.
   C. If turning six years old, Jim's uncle would teach Spanish to him.
   D. Fax a copy of your resume to Ms. Perez and me.

1.____

2. A. Jerry stood in line for almost two hours.
   B. The reaction to my engagement was less exciting than I thought it would be.
   C. Carlos and me have done great work on this project.
   D. Two parts of the speech needs to be revised before tomorrow.

2.____

3. A. Arriving home, the alarm was tripped.
   B. Jonny is regarded as a stand up guy, a responsible parent, and he doesn't give up until a task is finished.
   C. Each employee must submit a drug test each month.
   D. One of the documents was incinerated in the explosion.

3.____

4. A. As soon as my parents get home, I told them I finished all of my chores.
   B. I asked my teacher to send me my missing work, check my absences, and how did I do on my test.
   C. Matt attempted to keep it concealed from Jenny and me.
   D. If Mary or him cannot get work done on time, I will have to split them up.

4.____

5. A. Driving to work, the traffic report warned him of an accident on Highway 47.
   B. Jimmy has performed well this season.
   C. Since finishing her degree, several job offers have been given to Cam.
   D. Our boss is creating unstable conditions for we employees.

5.____

6. A. The thief was described as a tall man with a wiry mustache weighing approximately 150 pounds.
   B. She gave Patrick and I some more time to finish our work.
   C. One of the books that he ordered was damaged in shipping.
   D. While talking on the rotary phone, the car Jim was driving skidded off the road.

6.____

2 (#4)

Questions 7-9.

DIRECTIONS: Questions 7 through 9 are to be answered on the basis of the following graph.

Ice Lake Frozen Flight (2002-2013)		
Year	Number of Participants	Temperature (Fahrenheit)
2002	22	4°
2003	50	33°
2004	69	18°
2005	104	22°
2006	108	24°
2007	288	33°
2008	173	9°
2009	598	39°
2010	698	26°
2011	696	30°
2012	777	28°
2013	578	32°

7. Which two year span had the LARGEST difference between temperatures?   7.____
   A. 2002 and 2003
   B. 2011 and 2012
   C. 2008 and 2009
   D. 2003 and 2004

8. How many total people participated in the years after the temperature reached at least 29°°?   8.____
   A. 2,295
   B. 1,717
   C. 2,210
   D. 4,543

9. In 2007, the event saw 288 participants, while in 2008 that number dropped to 173. Which of the following reasons BEST explains the drop in participants?   9.____
   A. The event had not been going on that long and people didn't know about it.
   B. The lake water wasn't cold enough to have people jump in.
   C. The temperature was too cold for many people who would have normally participated.
   D. None of the above reasons explain the drop in participants.

10. In the following list of numbers, how many times does 4 come just after 2 when 2 comes just after an odd number?   10.____
    2365247653898632488572486392424
    A. 2
    B. 3
    C. 4
    D. 5

11. Which choice below lists the letter that is as far after B as S is after N in the alphabet?   11.____
    A. G
    B. H
    C. I
    D. J

Questions 12-15.

DIRECTIONS: Questions 12 through 15 are to be answered on the basis of the following directory and list of changes.

Directory		
Name	Emp. Type	Position
Julie Taylor	Warehouse	Packer
James King	Office	Administrative Assistant
John Williams	Office	Salesperson
Ray Moore	Warehouse	Maintenance
Kathleen Byrne	Warehouse	Supervisor
Amy Jones	Office	Salesperson
Paul Jonas	Office	Salesperson
Lisa Wong	Warehouse	Loader
Eugene Lee	Office	Accountant
Bruce Lavine	Office	Manager
Adam Gates	Warehouse	Packer
Will Suter	Warehouse	Packer
Gary Lorper	Office	Accountant
Jon Adams	Office	Salesperson
Susannah Harper	Office	Salesperson

Directory Updates:
- Employee e-mail addresses will adhere to the following guidelines: lastnamefirstname@apexindustries.com (ex. Susannah Harper is harpersusannah@apexindustries.com). Currently, employees in the warehouse share one e-mail, distribution@apexindustries.com.
- The "Loader" position will now be referred to as "Specialist I"
- Adam Gates has accepted a Supervisor position within the Warehouse and is no longer a Packer. All warehouse employees report to the two Supervisors and all office employees report to the Manager.

12. Amy Jones tried to send an e-mail to Adam Gates, but it wouldn't send. Which of the following offers the BEST explanation? 12.____
    A. Amy put Adam's first name first and then his last name.
    B. Adam doesn't check his e-mail, so he wouldn't know if he received the e-mail or not.
    C. Adam does not have his own e-mail.
    D. Office employees are not allowed to send e-mails to each other.

13. How many Packers currently work for Apex Industries? 13.____
    A. 2   B. 3   C. 4   D. 5

14. What position does Lisa Wong currently hold? 14.____
    A. Specialist I   B. Secretary
    C. Administrative Assistant   D. Loader

15. If an employee wanted to contact the office manager, which of the following e-mails should the e-mail be sent to? 15.____
    A. officemanager@apexindustries.com
    B. brucelavine@apexindustries.com
    C. lavinebruce@apexindustries.com
    D. distribution@apexindustries.com

Questions 16-19.

DIRECTIONS: In answering Questions 16 through 19, compare the three names, numbers or addresses.

16. Smiley Yarnell   Smiley Yarnel   Smily Yarnell   16.____
    A. All three are exactly alike.
    B. The first and second are exactly alike.
    C. The second and third are exactly alike.
    D. All three are different.

17. 1583 Theater Drive   1583 Theater Drive   1583 Theatre Drive   17.____
    A. All three are exactly alike.
    B. The first and second are exactly alike.
    C. The second and third are exactly alike.
    D. All three are different.

18. 3341893212   3341893212   3341893212   18.____
    A. All three are exactly alike.
    B. The first and second are exactly alike.
    C. The second and third are exactly alike.
    D. All three are different.

19. Douglass Watkins   Douglas Watkins   Douglass Watkins   19.____
    A. All three are exactly alike.
    B. The first and third are exactly alike.
    C. The second and third are exactly alike.
    D. All three are different.

Questions 20-24.

DIRECTIONS: In answering Questions 20 through 24, you will be presented with a word. Choose the synonym that BEST represents the word in question.

20. Flexible   20.____
    A. delicate   B. inflammable   C. strong   D. pliable

21. Alternative   21.____
    A. choice   B. moderate   C. lazy   D. value

22. Corroborate 22.____
    A. examine   B. explain   C. verify   D. explain

23. Respiration 23.____
    A. recovery   B. breathing C. sweating D. selfish

24. Negligent 24.____
    A. lazy   B. moderate   C. hopeless D. lax

25. Plumber is to Wrench as Painter is to 25.____
    A. pipe   B. shop   C. hammer   D. brush

KEY (CORRECT ANSWERS)

1. D
2. A
3. D
4. C
5. B

6. C
7. C
8. B
9. C
10. C

11. A
12. C
13. A
14. A
15. C

16. D
17. B
18. A
19. B
20. D

21. A
22. C
23. B
24. D
25. D

NAME AND NUMBER CHECKING
EXAMINATION SECTION
TEST 1

DIRECTIONS: This test is designed to measure your speed/and accuracy. You are urged to work both quickly and accurately and to do correctly as many lists as you can in the time allowed. The test consists of lists or pairs of names and numbers. Count the number of IDENTICAL pairs in each list. Then, select the correct number, 1, 2, 3, 4, 5, and indicate your choice in the space at the right. Two sample questions are presented for your guidance, together with the correct solutions.

SAMPLE LIST A
Adelphi College – Adelphia College
Braxton Corp – Braxeton Corp.
Wassaic State School – Wassaic State School
Central Islip State Hospital – Central Isllip State Hospital
Greenwich House – Greenwich House

NOTE: There are only two correct pairs—Wassaic State School and Greenwich House. Therefore, the CORRECT answer is 2.

SAMPLE LIST B
78453694 – 78453684
784530 – 784530
533 – 534
67845 – 67845
2368745 – 2368755

NOTE: There are only two correct pairs—784530 and 67845. Therefore, the CORRECT answer is 2.

LIST 1   1._____
    Diagnostic Clinic   – Diagnostic Clinic
    Yorkville Health   – Yorkville Health
    Meinhard Clinic   – Meinhart Clinic
    Corlears Clinic   – Carlears Clinic
    Tremont Diagnostic   – Tremont Diagnostic

LIST 2   2._____
    73526   – 73526
    7283627198   – 7283627198
    627   – 637
    728352617283   – 7283526178282
    6281   – 6281

2 (#1)

LIST 3   3.____
    Jefferson Clinic   – Jeffersen Clinic
    Mott Haven Center   – Mott Havan Center
    Bronx Hospital   – Bronx Hospital
    Montefiore Hospital   – Montifeore Hospital
    Beth Isreal Hospital   – Beth Israel Hospital

LIST 4   4.____
    936271826   – 936371826
    5271   – 5291
    82637192037   – 82637192037
    527182   – 5271882
    726354256   - 72635456

LIST 5   5.____
    Trinity Hospital   – Trinity Hospital
    Central Harlem   – Centrel Harlem
    St. Luke's Hospital – St. Lukes' Hospital
    Mt. Sinai Hospital   – Mt. Sinia Hospital
    N.Y. Dispensery   – N.Y. Dispensary

LIST 6   6.____
    725361552637   – 725361555637
    7526378   – 7526377
    6975   – 6975
    82637481028   – 82637481028
    3427   – 3429

LIST 7   7.____
    Misericordia Hospital – Miseracordia Hospital
    Lebonan Hospital   – Lebanon Hospital
    Gouverneur Hospital – Gouverner Hospital
    German Polyclinic   – German Policlinic
    French Hospital   – French Hospital

LIST 8   8.____
    8277364933251   – 827364933351
    63728   – 63728
    367281   – 367281
    62733846273   – 6273846293
    62836   - 6283

LIST 9   9.____
    King's County Hospital – Kings County Hospital
    St. Johns Long Island – St. John's Long Island
    Bellevue Hospital   – Bellvue Hospital
    Beth David Hospital   – Beth David Hospital
    Samaritan Hospital   – Samariton Hospital

3 (#1)

LIST 10   10.____
    62836454   – 62836455
    42738267   – 42738369
    573829   – 573829
    738291627874   – 738291627874
    725   - 735

LIST 11   11.____
    Bloomingdal Clinic   – Bloomingdale Clinic
    Communitty Hospital   – Community Hospital
    Metroplitan Hospital   – Metropoliton Hospital
    Lenox Hill Hospital   – Lonex Hill Hospital
    Lincoln Hospital   – Lincoln Hospital

LIST 12   12.____
    6283364728   – 6283648
    627385   – 627383
    54283902   – 54283602
    63354   – 63354
    7283562781   - 7283562781

LIST 13   13.____
    Sydenham Hospital   – Sydanham Hospital
    Roosevalt Hospital   – Roosevelt Hospital
    Vanderbilt Clinic   – Vanderbild Clinic
    Women's Hospital   – Woman's Hospital
    Flushing Hospital   – Flushing Hospital

LIST 14   14.____
    62738   – 62738
    727355542321   – 72735542321
    263849332   – 263849332
    262837   – 263837
    47382912   - 47382922

LIST 15   15.____
    Episcopal Hospital   – Episcapal Hospital
    Flower Hospital   – Flouer Hospital
    Stuyvesent Clinic   – Stuyvesant Clinic
    Jamaica Clinic   – Jamaica Clinic
    Ridgwood Clinic   – Ridgewood Clinic

LIST 16   16.____
    628367299   – 628367399
    111   – 111
    118293304829   – 1182839489
    4448   – 4448
    333693678   - 333693678

LIST 17
- Arietta Crane Farm — Areitta Crane Farm
- Bikur Chilim Home — Bikur Chilom Home
- Burke Foundation — Burke Foundation
- Blythedale Home — Blythdale Home
- Campbell Cottages — Cambell Cottages

17.____

LIST 18
- 32123 — 32132
- 273893326783 — 27389326783
- 473829 — 473829
- 7382937 — 7383937
- 3628890122332 — 36289012332

18.____

LIST 19
- Caraline Rest — Caroline Rest
- Loreto Rest — Loretto Rest
- Edgewater Creche — Edgwater Creche
- Holiday Farm — Holiday Farm
- House of St. Giles — House of st. Giles

19.____

LIST 20
- 557286777 — 55728677
- 3678902 — 3678892
- 1567839 — 1567839
- 7865434712 — 7865344712
- 9927382 — 9927382

20.____

LIST 21
- Isabella Home — Isabela Home
- James A. Moore Home — James A. More Home
- The Robin's Nest — The Roben's Nest
- Pelham Home — Pelam Home
- St. Eleanora's Home — St. Eleanora's Home

21.____

LIST 22
- 273648293048 — 273648293048
- 334 — 334
- 7362536478 — 7362536478
- 7362819273 — 7362819273
- 7362 — 7363

22.____

LIST 23
- St. Pheobe's Mission — St. Phebe's Mission
- Seaside Home — Seaside Home
- Speedwell Society — Speedwell Society
- Valeria Home — Valera Home
- Wiltwyck — Wildwyck

23.____

5 (#1)

LIST 24   24._____
 63728   – 63738
 63728192736 – 63728192738
 428   – 458
 62738291527 – 62738291529
 63728192   - 63728192

LIST 25   25._____
 McGaffin   – McGafin
 David Ardslee – David Ardslee
 Axton Supply – Axeton Supply Co
 Alice Russell – Alice Russell
 Dobson Mfg. Co. – Dobsen Mfg. Co.

KEY (CORRECT ANSWERS)

1.	3		11.	1
2.	3		12.	2
3.	1		13.	1
4.	1		14.	2
5.	1		15.	1
6.	2		16.	3
7.	1		17.	1
8.	2		18.	1
9.	1		19.	1
10.	2		20.	2

21.	1
22.	4
23.	2
24.	1
25.	2

TEST 2

DIRECTIONS: This test is designed to measure your speed/and accuracy. You are urged to work both quickly and accurately and to do correctly as many lists as you can in the time allowed. The test consists of lists or pairs of names and numbers. Count the number of IDENTICAL pairs in each list. Then, select the correct number, 1, 2, 3, 4, 5, and indicate your choice in the space at the right.

LIST 1
 82637381028   – 82637281028
 928   – 928
 72937281028   – 72937281028
 7362   – 7362
 927382615   – 927382615

1.____

LIST 2
 Albee Theatre   – Albee Theatre
 Lapland Lumber Co.   – Laplund Lumber Co.
 Adelphi College   – Adelphi College
 Jones & Son Inc.   – Jones & Sons Inc.
 S.W. Ponds Co.   – S.W. Ponds Co.

2.____

LIST 3
 85345   – 85345
 895643278   – 895643277
 726352   – 726353
 632685   – 632685
 7263524   – 7236524

3.____

LIST 4
 Eagle Library   – Eagle Library
 Dodge Ltd.   – Dodge Co.
 Stromberg Carlson   – Stromberg Carlsen
 Clairice Ling   – Clairice Linng
 Mason Book Co.   – Matson Book Co.

4.____

LIST 5
 66273   – 66273
 629   – 629
 7382517283   – 7382517283
 637281   – 639281
 2738261   – 2788261

5.____

LIST 6
 Robert MacColl   – Robert McColl
 Buick Motor   – Buck Motors
 Murray Bay & Co. Ltd.   – Murray Bay Co. Ltd.
 L.T. Ltyle   – L.T. Lyttle
 A.S. Landas   – A.S. Landas

6.____

2 (#2)

LIST 7   7.____
    6271526374890   – 627152637490
    73526189   – 73526189
    5372   – 5392
    637281142   – 63728124
    4783946   – 4783046

LIST 8   8.____
    Tyndall Burke   – Tyndell Burke
    W. Briehl   – W. Briehl
    Burritt Publishing Co. – Buritt Publishing Co.
    Frederick Breyer & Co. – Frederick Breyer Co.
    Bailey Buulard   – Bailey Bullard

LIST 9   9.____
    634   – 634
    16837   – 163837
    273892223678   – 27389223678
    527182   – 527782
    3628901223   – 3629002223

LIST 10   10.____
    Ernest Boas   – Ernest Boas
    Rankin Barne   – Rankin Barnes
    Edward Appley   – Edward Appely
    Camel   – Camel
    Caiger Food Co.   – Caiger Food Co.

LIST 11   11.____
    6273   – 6273
    322   – 332
    15672839   – 15672839
    63728192637   – 63728192639
    738   – 738

LIST 12   12.____
    Wells Fargo Co.   – Wells Fargo Co.
    W.D. Brett   – W.D. Britt
    Tassco Co.   – Tassko Co.
    Republic Mills   – Republic Mill
    R.W. Burnham   – R.W. Burhnam

LIST 13   13.____
    7253529152   – 7283529152
    6283   – 6383
    52839102738   – 5283910238
    308   – 398
    82637201927   – 8263720127

LIST 14
  Schumacker Co.   – Shumacker Co.
  C.H. Caiger   – C.H. Caiger
  Abraham Strauss   – Abram Straus
  B.F. Boettjer   – B.F. Boettijer
  Cut-Rate Store   – Cut-Rate Stores

14.____

LIST 15
  15273826   – 15273826
  72537   – 73537
  726391027384   – 62639107384
  637389   – 627399
  725382910   – 725382910

15.____

LIST 16
  Hixby Ltd.   – Hixby Lt'd.
  S. Reiner   – S. Riener
  Reynard Co.   – Reynord Co.
  Esso Gassoline Co. – Esso Gasolene Co.
  Belle Brock   – Belle Brock

16.____

LIST 17
  7245   – 7245
  819263728192   – 819263728172
  682537289   – 682537298
  789   – 789
  82936542891   – 82936542891

17.____

LIST 18
  Joseph Cartwright   – Joseph Cartwrite
  Foote Food Co.   – Foot Food Co.
  Weiman & Held   – Weiman & Held
  Sanderson Shoe Co. – Sandersen Shoe Co.
  A.M. Byrne   – A.N. Byrne

18.____

LIST 19
  4738267   – 4738277
  63728   – 63729
  6283628901   – 6283628991
  918264   – 918264
  263728192037   – 2637728192073

19.____

LIST 20
  Exray Laboratories – Exray Labratories
  Curley Toy Co.   – Curly Toy Co.
  J. Lauer & Cross   – J. Laeur & Cross
  Mireco Brands   – Mireco Brands
  Sandor Lorand   – Sandor Larand

20.____

4 (#2)

LIST 21   21.____
    607   – 609
    6405   – 6403
    976   – 996
    101267   – 101267
    2065432   – 20965432

LIST 22   22.____
    John Macy & Sons   – John Macy & Son
    Venus Pencil Co.   – Venus Pencil Co.
    Nell McGinnis   – Nell McGinnis
    McCutcheon & Co.   – McCutcheon & Co.
    Sun-Tan Oil   – Sun-Tan Oil

LIST 23   23.____
    703345700   – 703345700
    46754   – 466754
    3367490   – 3367490
    3379   – 3778
    47384   – 47394

LIST 24   24.____
    arthritis   – arthritis
    asthma   – asthma
    endocrine   – endocrene
    gastro-enterological – gastrol-enteralogical
    orthopedic   – orthopedic

LIST 25   25.____
    743829432   – 743828432
    998   – 998
    732816253902   – 732816252902
    46829   – 46830
    7439120249   – 7439210249

KEY (CORRECT ANSWERS)

1.	4		11.	3
2.	3		12.	1
3.	2		13.	1
4.	1		14.	1
5.	2		15.	2
6.	1		16.	1
7.	2		17.	3
8.	1		18.	1
9.	1		19.	1
10.	3		20.	1

21.	1
22.	4
23.	2
24.	3
25.	1

NAME AND NUMBER COMPARISONS

COMMENTARY

This test seeks to measure your ability and disposition to do a job carefully and accurately, your attention to exactness and preciseness of detail, your alertness and versatility in discerning similarities and differences between things, and your power in systematically handling written language symbols.

It is actually a test of your ability to do academic and/or clerical work, using the basic elements of verbal (qualitative) and mathematical (quantitative) learning—words and numbers.

EXAMINATION SECTION

TEST 1

DIRECTIONS: In each line across the page there are three names or numbers that are much alike. Compare the three names or numbers and decide which ones are exactly alike. *PRINT IN THE SPACE AT THE RIGHT THE LETTER:*
A. if all THREE names or numbers are exactly alike
B. if only the FIRST and SECOND names or numbers are ALIKE
C. if only the FIRST and THIRD names or numbers are alike
D. if only the SECOND or THIRD names or numbers are alike
E. if ALL THREE names or numbers are DIFFERENT

1.	Davis Hazen	David Hozen	David Hazen	1.____
2.	Lois Appel	Lois Appel	Lois Apfel	2.____
3.	June Allan	Jane Allan	Jane Allan	3.____
4.	10235	10235	10235	4.____
5.	32614	32164	32614	5.____

TEST 2

1.	2395890	2395890	2395890	1.____
2.	1926341	1926347	1926314	2.____
3.	E. Owens McVey	E. Owen McVey	E. Owen McVay	3.____
4.	Emily Neal Rouse	Emily Neal Rowse	Emily Neal Rowse	4.____
5.	H. Merritt Audubon	H. Merriott Audubon	H. Merritt Audubon	5.____

TEST 3

1. 6219354	6219354	6219354	1.____
2. 231793	2312793	2312793	2.____
3. 1065407	1065407	1065047	3.____
4. Francis Ransdell	Frances Ramsdell	Francis Ramsdell	4.____
5. Cornelius Detwiler	Cornelius Detwiler	Cornelius Detwiler	5.____

TEST 4

1. 6452054	6452564	6542054	1.____
2. 8501268	8501268	8501286	2.____
3. Ella Burk Newham	Ella Burk Newnham	Elena Burk Newnham	3.____
4. Jno. K. Ravencroft	Jno. H. Ravencroft	Jno. H. Ravencoft	4.____
5. Martin Wills Pullen	Martin Wills Pulen	Martin Wills Pullen	5.____

TEST 5

1. 3457988	3457986	3457986	1.____
2. 4695682	4695862	4695682	2.____
3. Stricklund Kaneydy	Sticklund Kanedy	Stricklund Kanedy	3.____
4. Joy Harlor Witner	Joy Harloe Witner	Joy Harloe Witner	4.____
5. R.M.O. Uberroth	R.M.O. Uberroth	R.N.O. Uberroth	5.____

TEST 6

1.	1592514	1592574	1592574	1.____
2.	2010202	2010202	2010220	2.____
3.	6177396	6177936	6177396	3.____
4.	Drusilla S. Ridgeley	Drusilla S. Ridgeley	Drusilla S. Ridgeley	4.____
5.	Andrei I. Tooumantzev	Andrei I. Tourmantzev	Andrei I. Toumantzov	5.____

TEST 7

1.	5261383	5261383	5261338	1.____
2.	8125690	8126690	8125609	2.____
3.	W.E. Johnston	W.E. Johnson	W.E. Johnson	3.____
4.	Vergil L. Muller	Vergil L. Muller	Vergil L. Muller	4.____
5.	Atherton R. Warde	Asheton R. Warde	Atherton P. Warde	5.____

TEST 8

1.	013469.5	023469.5	02346.95	1.____
2.	33376	333766	333766	2.____
3.	Ling-Temco-Vought	Ling-Tenco-Vought	Ling-Temco Vought	3.____
4.	Lorilard Corp.	Lorillard Corp.	Lorrilard Corp.	4.____
5.	American Agronomics Corporation	American Agronomics Corporation	American Agronomic Corporation	5.____

TEST 9

1.	436592864	436592864	436592864	1.	____
2.	197765123	197755123	197755123	2.	____
3.	Dewaay Cortvriendt International S.A.	Deway Cortvriendt International S.A.	Deway Corturiendt International S.A.	3.	____
4.	Crèdit Lyonnais	Crèdit Lyonnais	Crèdit Lyonais	4.	____
5.	Algemene Bank Nederland N.V.	Algamene Bank Nederland N.V.	Algemene Bank Naderland N.V.	5.	____

TEST 10

1.	00032572	0.0032572	00032522	1.	____
2.	399745	399745	398745	2.	____
3.	Banca Privata Finanziaria S.p.A.	Banca Privata Finanzaria S.P.A.	Banca Privata Finanziaria S.P.A.	3.	____
4.	Eastman Dillon, Union Securities & Co.	Eastman Dillon, Union Securities Co.	Eastman Dillon, Union Securities & Co.	4.	____
5.	Arnhold and S. Bleichroeder, Inc.	Arnhold & S. Bleichroeder, Inc.	Arnold and S. Bleichroeder, Inc.	5.	____

TEST 11

DIRECTIONS: Answer the questions below on the basis of the following instructions: For each such numbered set of names, addresses, and numbers listed in Columns I and II, select your answer from the following options:
A. The names in Columns I and II are different
B. The addresses in Columns I and II are different
C. The numbers in Columns I and II are different
D. The names, addresses and numbers are identical

1. Francis Jones
   62 Stately Avenue
   96-12446

   Francis Jones
   62 Stately Avenue
   96-21446

   1.____

2. Julio Montez
   19 Ponderosa Road
   56-73161

   Julio Montez
   19 Ponderosa Road
   56-71361

   2.____

3. Mary Mitchell
   2314 Melbourne Drive
   68-92172

   Mary Mitchell
   2314 Melbourne Drive
   68-92172

   3.____

4. Harry Patterson
   25 Dunne Street
   14-33430

   Harry Patterson
   25 Dunne Street
   14-34330

   4.____

5. Patrick Murphy
   171 West Hosmer Street
   93-81214

   Patrick Murphy
   171 West Hosmer Street
   93-18214

   5.____

TEST 12

1. August Schultz
   816 St. Clair Avenue
   53-40149

   August Schultz
   816 St. Claire Avenue
   53-40149

   1.____

2. George Taft
   72 Runnymede Street
   47-04033

   George Taft
   72 Runnymede Street
   47-04023

   2.____

3. Angus Henderson
   1418 Madison Street
   81-76375

   Angus Henderson
   1418 Madison Street
   81-76375

   3.____

4. Carolyn Mazur
   12 Rivenlew Road
   38-99615

   Carolyn Mazur
   12 Rivervane Road
   38-99615

   4.____

5. Adele Russell
   1725 Lansing Lane
   72-91962

   Adela Russell
   1725 Lansing Lane
   72-91962

   5.____

TEST 13

DIRECTIONS: The following questions are based on the instructions given below. In each of the following questions, the 3-line name and address in Column I is the master-list entry, and the 3-line entry in Column II is the information to be checked against the master list.
If there is one line that is NOT exactly alike, mark your answer A.
If there are two lines NOT exactly alike, mark your answer B.
If there are three lines NOT exactly alike, mark your answer C.
If the lines ALL are exactly alike, mark your answer D.

1. Jerome A. Jackson
   1243 14th Avenue
   New York, N.Y. 10023

   Jerome A. Johnson
   1234 14th Avenue
   New York, N.Y. 10023

   1.____

2. Sophie Strachtheim
   33-28 Connecticut Ave.
   Far Rockaway, N.Y. 11697

   Sophie Strachtheim
   33-28 Connecticut Ave.
   Far Rockaway, N.Y. 11697

   2.____

3. Elisabeth NT. Gorrell
   256 Exchange St
   New York, N.Y. 10013

   Elizabeth NT. Correll
   256 Exchange St.
   New York, N.Y. 10013

   3.____

4. Maria J. Gonzalez
   7516 E. Sheepshead Rd.
   Brooklyn, N.Y. 11240

   Maria J. Gonzalez
   7516 N. Shepshead Rd.
   Brooklyn, N.Y. 11240

   4.____

5. Leslie B. Brautenweiler
   21-57A Seller Terr.
   Flushing, N.Y. 11367

   Leslie B. Brautenwieler
   21-75ASeiler Terr.
   Flushing, N.J. 11367

   5.____

KEY (CORRECT ANSWERS)

TEST 1	TEST 2	TEST 3	TEST 4	TEST 5	TEST 6	TEST 7
1. E	1. A	1. A	1. E	1. D	1. D	1. B
2. B	2. E	2. A	2. B	2. C	2. B	2. E
3. D	3. E	3. B	3. E	3. E	3. C	3. D
4. A	4. D	4. E	4. E	4. D	4. A	4. A
5. C	5. C	5. A	5. C	5. B	5. E	5. E

TEST 8	TEST 9	TEST 10	TEST 11	TEST 12	TEST 13
1. E	1. A	1. E	1. C	1. B	1. B
2. D	2. D	2. B	2. C	2. C	2. D
3. E	3. E	3. E	3. D	3. D	3. A
4. E	4. E	4. C	4. C	4. B	4. A
5. B	5. E	5. E	5. C	5. A	5. C

CODING

COMMENTARY

An ingenious question-type called coding, involving elements of alphabetizing, filing, name and number comparison, and evaluative judgment and application, has currently won wide acceptance in testing circles for measuring clerical aptitude and general ability, particularly on the senior (middle) grades (levels).

While the directions for this question-type usually vary in detail, the candidate is generally asked to consider groups of names, codes, and numbers, and, then, according to a given plan, to arrange codes in alphabetic order; to arrange these in numerical sequence; to re-arrange columns of names and numbers in correct order; to espy errors in coding; to choose the correct coding arrangement in consonance with the given directions and examples, etc.

This question-type appears to have few parameters in respect to form, substance, or degree of difficulty.

Accordingly, acquaintance with, and practice in the coding question is recommended for the serious candidate.

EXAMINATION SECTION
TEST 1

DIRECTIONS: Questions 1 through 10 are to be answered on the basis of the following Code Table. In this table every letter has a corresponding code number to be punched. Each question contains three lines of letters and code numbers. In each line, the code numbers should correspond with the letters in accordance with the table.

Letter	M	X	R	T	W	A	E	Q	Z	C
Code	1	2	3	4	5	6	7	8	9	0

On some of the lines, an error exists in the coding. Compare the letters and numbers in each question carefully. If you find an error or errors on
    only *one* of the lines in the question, mark your answer A;
    any *two* lines in the question, mark your answer B;
    all *three* lines in the question, mark your answer C;
    none of the lines in the question, mark your answer D.

SAMPLE QUESTION

    XAQMZMRQ   -   26819138
    RAERQEX   -   3573872
    TMZCMTZA   -   46901496

In the above sample, the first line is correct since each letter, as listed, has the correct corresponding code number.
In the second line, an error exists because the letter A should have the code number 6 instead of 5.
In the third line, an error exists because the letter W should have the code number 5 instead of 6.
Since there are errors in two of the three lines, your answer should be B.

1.   EQRMATTR - 78316443
   MACWXRQW - 16052385
   XZEMCAR   - 2971063

2.   CZEMRXQ   - 0971238
   XMTARET   - 2146374
   WCEARWEC - 50863570

3.   CEXAWRQZ - 07265389
   RCRMMZQT - 33011984
   ACMZWTEX - 60195472

4.   XRCZQZWR - 23089953
   CMRQCAET - 01389574
   ZXRWTECM - 92345701

1._____
2._____
3._____
4._____

5. AXMTRAWR   -   62134653   5. ____
    EQQCZCEW   -   77809075
    MAZQARTM   -   16086341

6. WRWQCTRM   -   53580431   6. ____
    CXMWAERZ   -   02156739
    RCQEWWME   -   30865517

7. CRMECEAX   -   03170762   7. ____
    MZCTRXRQ   -   19043238
    XXZREMEW   -   22937175

8. MRCXQEAX   -   13928762   8. ____
    WAMZTRMZ   -   65194319
    ECXARWXC   -   70263520

9. MAWXECRQ   -   16527038   9. ____
    RXQEAETM   -   32876741
    RXEWMCZQ   -   32751098

10. MRQZCATE   -   13890647   10. ____
    WCETRXAW   -   50743625
    CZWMCERT   -   09510734

KEY (CORRECT ANSWERS)

1. D
2. B
3. A
4. C
5. C

6. A
7. D
8. B
9. D
10. A

TEST 2

DIRECTIONS: Questions 1 through 6 consist of three lines of code letters and numbers. The numbers on each, line should correspond with the code letters on the same line in accordance with the table below.

Code Letter	F	X	L	M	R	W	T	S	B	H
Corresponding Number	0	1	2	3	4	5	6	7	8	9

On some of the lines, an error exists in the coding. Compare the letters and numbers in each question carefully. If you find an error or errors on
    only *one* of the lines in the question, mark your answer A;
    any *two* lines in the question, mark your answer B;
    all *three* lines in the question, mark your answer C;
    none of the lines in the question, mark your answer D.

SAMPLE QUESTION

    LTSXHMF   2671930
    TBRWHLM   6845913
    SXLBFMR   5128034

In the above sample, the first line is correct since each code letter listed has the correct corresponding number.
    On the second line, an error exists because code letter L should have the number 2 instead of the number 1.
    On the third line, an error exists because the code letter S should have the number 7 instead of the number 5.
    Since there are errors on two of the three lines, the correct answer is B.

1. XMWBHLR   1358924
   FWSLRHX   0572491
   MTXBLTS   3618267

2. XTLSMRF   1627340
   BMHRFLT   8394026
   HLTSWRX   9267451

3. LMBSFXS   2387016
   RWLMBSX   4532871
   SMFXBHW   7301894

4. RSTWTSML   47657632
   LXRMHFBS   21439087
   FTLBMRWX   06273451

5. XSRSBWFM   17478603
   BRMXRMXT   84314216
   XSTFBWRL   17609542

6. TMSBXHLS 63781927
   RBSFLFWM 48702053
   MHFXWTRS 39015647

6.____

KEY (CORRECT ANSWERS)

1. D
2. A
3. C
4. B
5. C
6. D

TEST 3

DIRECTIONS: Questions 1 through 5 consist of three lines of code letters and numbers. The numbers on each line should correspond with the code letters on the same line in accordance with the table below.

Code Letter	P	L	I	J	B	O	H	U	C	G
Corresponding Number	0	1	2	3	4	5	6	7	8	9

On some of the lines, an error exists in the coding. Compare the letters and numbers in each question carefully. If you find an error or errors on
    only *one* of the lines in the question, mark your answer A;
    any *two* lines in the question, mark your answer B;
    all *three* lines in the question, mark your answer C;
    none of the lines in the question, mark your answer D.

SAMPLE QUESTION

    JHOILCP   3652180
    BICLGUP   4286970
    UCIBHLJ   5824613

In the above sample, the first line is correct since each code letter listed has the correct corresponding number.
On the second line, an error exists because code letter L should have the number 1 instead of the number 6.
On the third line an error exists because the code letter U should have the number 7 instead of the number 5.
Since there are errors on two of the three lines, the correct answer is B.

1.   BULJCIP   4713920
   HIGPOUL   6290571
   OCUHJBI   5876342

2.   CUBLOIJ   8741023
   LCLGCLB   1818914
   JPUHIOC   3076158

3.   OIJGCBPO   52398405
   UHPBLIOP   76041250
   CLUIPGPC   81720908

4.   BPCOUOJI   40875732
   UOHCIPLB   75682014
   GLHUUCBJ   92677843

5.   HOIOHJLH   65256361
   IOJJHHBP   25536640
   OJHBJOPI   53642502

KEY (CORRECT ANSWERS)

1. A
2. C
3. D
4. B
5. C

TEST 4

DIRECTIONS: Questions 1 through 5 consist of three lines of code letters and numbers. The numbers on each line should correspond with the code letters on the same line in accordance with the table below.

Code Letters	Q	S	L	Y	M	O	U	N	W	Z
Corresponding Numbers	1	2	3	4	5	6	7	8	9	0

On some of the lines, an error exists in the coding. Compare the letters and numbers in each question carefully. If you find an error on

only *one* of the lines in the question, mark your answer A;
any *two* lines in the question, mark your answer B;
all *three* lines in the question, mark your answer C;
none of the lines in the question, mark your answer D.

SAMPLE QUESTION
MOQNWZQS   56189012
QWNMOLYU   19865347
LONLMYWN   36835489

In the above sample, the first line is correct since each code letter, as listed, has the correct corresponding number.
On the second line, an error exists because code letter M should have the number 5 instead of the number 6.
On the third line an error exists because the code letter W should have the number 9 instead of the number 8.
Since there are errors on two of the three lines, the correct answer is B.

1. SMUWOLQN   25796318   1._____
   ULSQNMZL   73218503
   NMYQZUSL   85410723

2. YUWWMYQZ   47995410   2._____
   SOSOSQSO   26262126
   ZUNLWMYW   07839549

3. QULSWZYN   17329045   3._____
   ZYLQWOYF   04319639
   QLUYWZSO   13749026

4. NLQZOYUM   83106475   4._____
   SQMUWZOM   21579065
   MMYWMZSQ   55498021

5. NQLOWZZU   81319007   5._____
   SMYLUNZO   25347806
   UWMSNZOL   79528013

KEY (CORRECT ANSWERS)

1. D
2. D
3. B
4. A
5. C

TEST 5

DIRECTIONS: Answer Questions 1 through 6 SOLELY on the basis of the chart and the instructions given below.

Toll Rate	$.25	$.30	$.45	$.60	$.75	$8.90	$1.20	$2.50
Classification Number of Vehicle	1	2	3	4	5	6	7	8

Assume that each of the amounts of money on the above chart is a toll rate charged for a type of vehicle and that the number immediately below each amount is the classification number for that type of vehicle. For instance, "1" is the classification number for a vehicle paying a $.25 toll; "2" is the classification number for a vehicle paying a $.30 toll; and so forth.

In each question, a series of tolls is given in Column I. Column II gives four different arrangements of classification numbers. You are to pick the answer (A, B, C, or D) in Column II that gives the classification numbers that match the tolls in Column I and are in the same order as the tolls in Column I.

SAMPLE QUESTION

Column I	Column II
$.30, $.90, $2.50, $.45	A. 2, 6, 8, 2
	B. 2, 8, 6, 3
	C. 2, 6, 8, 3
	D. 1, 6, 8, 3

According to the chart, the classification numbers that correspond to these toll rates are as follows: $.30 - 2, $.90 - 6, $2.50 - 8, $.45 - 3. Therefore, the right answer is 2, 6, 8, 3. The answer is C in Column II.

Do the following questions in the same way.

Column I | Column II

1. $.60, $.30, $.90, $1.20, $.60
   A. 4, 6, 2, 8, 4
   B. 4, 2, 6, 7, 4
   C. 2, 4, 7, 6, 2
   D. 2, 4, 6, 7, 4

2. $.90, $.45, $.25, $.45, $2.50, $.75
   A. 6, 3, 1, 3, 8, 3
   B. 6, 3, 3, 1, 8, 5
   C. 6, 1, 3, 3, 8, 5
   D. 6, 3, 1, 3, 8, 5

3. $.45, $.75, $1.20, $.25, $.25, $.30, $.45
   A. 3, 5, 7, 1, 1, 2, 3
   B. 5, 3, 7, 1, 1, 2, 3
   C. 3, 5, 7, 1, 2, 1, 3
   D. 3, 7, 5, 1, 1, 2, 3

4. $1.20, $2.50, $.45, $.90, $1.20, $.75, $.25
   A. 7, 8, 5, 6, 7, 5, 1
   B. 7, 8, 3, 7, 6, 5, 1
   C. 7, 8, 3, 6, 7, 5, 1
   D. 7, 8, 3, 6, 7, 1, 5

2 (#5)

5. $2.50, $1.20, $.90, $.25, $.60, $.45, $.30

   A. 8, 6, 7, 1, 4, 3, 2
   B. 8, 7, 5, 1, 4, 3, 2
   C. 8, 7, 6, 2, 4, 3, 2
   D. 8, 7, 6, 1, 4, 3, 2

5.___

6. $.75, $.25, $.45, $.60, $.90, $.30, $2.50

   A. 5, 1, 3, 2, 4, 6, 8
   B. 5, 1, 3, 4, 2, 6, 8
   C. 5, 1, 3, 4, 6, 2, 8
   D. 5, 3, 1, 4, 6, 2, 8

6.___

KEY (CORRECT ANSWERS)

1. B
2. D
3. A
4. C
5. D
6. C

TEST 6

DIRECTIONS: Answer Questions 1 through 10 on the basis of the following information:
A code number for any item is obtained by combining the date of delivery, number of units received, and number of units used. The first two digits represent the day of the month, the third and fourth digits represent the month, and the fifth and sixth digits represent the year.
The number following the letter R represents the number of units received and the number following the letter U represents the number of units used.
For example, the code number 120603-R5690-U1001 indicates that a delivery of 5,690 units was made on June 12, 2003 of which 1,001 units were used.

Questions 1-6.

DIRECTIONS: Using the chart below, answer Questions 1 through 6 by choosing the letter (A, B, C, or D) in which the supplier and stock number correspond to the code number given.

Supplier	Stock Number	Number of Units Received	Delivery Date	Number of Units Used
Stony	38390	8300	May 11, 2002	3800
Stoney	39803	1780	September 15, 2003	1703
Nievo	21220	5527	October 10, 2003	5007
Nieve	38903	1733	August 5, 2003	1703
Monte	39213	5527	October 10, 2002	5007
Stony	38890	3308	December 9, 2002	3300
Stony	83930	3880	September 12, 2002	380
Nevo	47101	485	June 11, 2002	231
Nievo	12122	5725	May 11, 2003	5201
Neve	47101	9721	August 15, 2003	8207
Nievo	21120	2275	January 7, 2002	2175
Rosa	41210	3821	March 3, 2003	2710
Stony	38890	3308	September 12, 2002	3300
Dinal	54921	1711	April 2, 2003	1117
Stony	33890	8038	March 5, 2003	3300
Dinal	54721	1171	March 2, 2002	717
Claridge	81927	3308	April 5, 2003	3088
Nievo	21122	4878	June 7, 2002	3492
Haley	39670	8300	December 23, 2003	5300

1. Code No. 120902-R3308-U3300   1.____

   A. Nievo - 12122   B. Stony - 83930
   C. Nievo - 21220   D. Stony -38890

2. Code No. 101002-R5527-U5007   2.____

   A. Nievo - 21220   B. Haley - 39670
   C. Monte - 39213   D. Claridge - 81927

3. Code No. 101003-R5527-U5007   3.____

   A. Nievo - 21220   B. Monte - 39213
   C. Nievo - 12122   D. Nievo - 21120

123

2 (#6)

4. Code No. 110503-R5725-U5201   4._____

   A. Nievo - 12122   B. Nievo - 21220
   C. Haley - 39670   D. Stony - 38390

5. Code No. 070102-R2275-U2175   5._____

   A. Stony - 33890   B. Stony - 83930
   C. Stony - 38390   D. Nievo - 21120

6. Code No. 120902-R3880-U380   6._____

   A. Stony - 83930   B. Stony - 38890
   C. Stony - 33890   D. Monte - 39213

Questions 7-10.

DIRECTIONS: Using the same chart, answer Questions 7 through 10 by choosing the letter (A, B, C, or D) in which the code number corresponds to the supplier and stock number given.

7. Nieve - 38903   7._____

   A. 851903-R1733-U1703   B. 080502-R1733-U1703
   C. 080503-R1733-U1703   D. 050803-R1733-U1703

8. Nevo - 47101   8._____

   A. 081503-R9721-U8207   B. 091503-R9721-U8207
   C. 110602-R485-U231   D. 061102-R485-U231

9. Dinal - 54921   9._____

   A. 020403-R1711-U1117   B. 030202-R1171-U717
   C. 020302-R1171-U717   D. 421903-R1711-U1117

10. Nievo - 21122   10._____

    A. 070602-R4878-U3492   B. 060702-R4878-U349
    C. 761902-R4878-U3492   D. 060702-R4878-U3492

KEY (CORRECT ANSWERS)

1. D
2. C
3. A
4. A
5. D

6. A
7. D
8. C
9. A
10. A

SPELLING
EXAMINATION SECTION
TEST 1

DIRECTIONS: In each of the following groups of words, only one of the words is misspelled. In each group, select the misspelled word and then write the letter of your choice in the answer space at the right.

1. A. cafeteria B. patron C. amateur D. perceive E. pledgeing 1.____

2. A. requirement B. financial C. accesory D. government E. college 2.____

3. A. approxamate B. mirror C. destroy D. disregard E. promising 3.____

4. A. sincerely B. discern C. wrangle D. truly E. audiovisual 4.____

5. A. tomatoes B. purity C. negligent D. dramatize E. plentiful! 5.____

6. A. theoretical B. seige C. C. volcano D. innocence E. dexterity 6.____

7. A. tommorrow B. reluctant C. shady D. unveil E. lightning 7.____

8. A. auction B. lenient C. prejudice D. sculpter E. originally 8.____

9. A. rhapsody B. perplex C. obtuse D. mortgage E. quandery 9.____

10. A. friendless B. hundreth C. singular D. channel E. attitude 10.____

11. A. missile B. propelled C. beautefy D. spirited E. spectacles 11.____

12. A. spaghetti B. missionery C. twelfth D. vegetable E. stifle 12.____

13. A. corrode B. hygiene C. irrelevant D. asociate E. maintenance 13.____

14. A. monogram B. minister C. criticle D. frequency E. genuine 14.____

15. A. introduce B. thematic C. economy D. valuable E. laborer 15.____

16. A. precede B. defalt C. heathen D. attain E. conscious 16.____

17. A. greivance B. chivalry C. scary 17.____

	D.	obscure	E.	pastime			
18.	A.	assurance	B.	immoderate	C.	patriotism	18.___
	D.	combustible	E.	stressfull			
19.	A.	inginuity	B.	legitimate	C.	schedule	19.___
	D.	accompanying	E.	substantial			
20.	A.	grafics	B.	merger	C.	global	20.___
	D.	sensitive	E.	exhibit			

KEY (CORRECT ANSWERS)

	CORRECT SPELLING			CORRECT SPELLING
1.	E, pledging		11.	C, beautify
2.	C, accessory		12.	B, missionary
3.	A, approximate		13.	D, associate
4.	D, truly		14.	C, critical
5.	E, plentiful		15.	E, laborer
6.	B, siege		16.	B, default
7.	A, tomorrow		17.	A, grievance
8.	D, sculptor		18.	E, stressful
9.	E, quandary		19.	A, ingenuity
10.	B, hundredth		20.	A, graphics

TEST 2

DIRECTIONS: In each of the following groups of words, only one of the words is misspelled. In each group, select the misspelled word and then write the letter of your choice in the answer space at the right.

1. A. pierce B. irritible C. ceiling 1.____
   D. portfolio E. hereditary

2. A. meanness B. anxious C. challange 2.____
   D. grief E. priority

3. A. anouncement B. politeness C. routine 3.____
   D. dependable E. bashful

4. A. scold B. pigeon C. transistor 4.____
   D. stomach E. decietful

5. A. antibiotic B. exagerate C. anticipation 5.____
   D. heavily E. essential

6. A. embarrass B. friendly C. diameter 6.____
   D. quite E. anguler

7. A. suffix B. persuade C. morgage 7.____
   D. exclusive E. pertinent

8. A. prologue B. gaseous C. stallion 8.____
   D. indevisible E. erroneous

9. A. acquarium B. tireless C. starred 9.____
   D. fried E. erroneous

10. A. innocent B. automatic C. reign 10.____
    D. primative E. substitute

11. A. satisfactory B. deceived C. existence 11.____
    D. anceint E. resolving

12. A. scandalize B. conferred C. aptitude 12.____
    D. spirited E. assurred

13. A. convenient B. already C. savage 13.____
    D. acheivement E. schedule

14. A. intercede B. cashier C. leisurely 14.____
    D. barameter E. interrelated

15. A. brittle B. freight C. rigidity 15.____
    D. tobacco E. excellance

16. A. ballet B. biscuit C. whimsecal 16.____
    D. inertia E. endeavor

17. A. intentionally B. mysterious C. nickel 17.____
    D. indicisive E. guarantee

129

18. A. occurred   B. calendar   C. sophmore   18.____
    D. extension   E. prevail

19. A. truant   B. syllabus   C. justifyable 19.____
    D. peasant   E. library

20. A. recomendation B. unanimous   C. symmetrical 20.____
    D. manageable   E. necessity

KEY (CORRECT ANSWERS)

		CORRECT SPELLING			CORRECT SPELLING
1.	B,	irritable	11.	D,	ancient
2.	C,	challenge	12.	E,	assured
3.	A,	announcement	13.	D,	achievement
4.	E,	deceitful	14.	D,	barometer
5.	B,	exaggerate	15.	E,	excellence
6.	E,	angular	16.	C,	whimsical
7.	C,	mortgage	17.	D,	indecisive
8.	D,	indivisible	18.	C,	sophomore
9.	A,	aquarium	19.	C,	justifiable
10.	D,	primitive	20.	A,	recommendation

TEST 3

DIRECTIONS: In each of the following groups of words, only one of the words is misspelled. In each group, select the misspelled word and then write the letter of your choice in the answer space at the right.

1. A. artillery B. patriotism C. fiery 1.____
   D. avalanche E. lieing

2. A. glossery B. omitted C. noticeable 2.____
   D. gaseous E. loveless

3. A. convocation B. particularly C. prevailing 3.____
   D. recollect E. impressonable

4. A. incompetent B. hereditery C. medicinal 4.____
   D. sustained E. turmoil

5. A. forgetting B. argument C. apparantly 5.____
   D. secrecy E. monopoly

6. A. against B. furthermore C. brief 6.____
   D. explore E. unanamous

7. A. suspision B. formerly C. opportunity 7.____
   D. concentrate E. intelligent

8. A. league B. analyze C. bribery 8.____
   D. usully E. straighten

9. A. rediculous B. recommend C. vengeance 9.____
   D. cemetery E. library

10. A. mountain B. percentage C. manageable 10.____
    D. unisen E. truly

11. A. caffeine B. tecnique C. invisible 11.____
    D. possession E. relieve

12. A. referral B. debtor C. shineing 12.____
    D. acceptable E. laborer

13. A. apology B. reputation C. sensible 13.____
    D. infansy E. eloquent

14. A. angrily B. umbrella C. observent 14.____
    D. fiend E. inquiry

15. A. earnest B. transfered C. responsible 15.____
    D. drunkenness E. portable

16. A. almanac B. entangle C. managing 16.____
    D. persistant E. indulge

17. A. exploit B. jewlery C. siege 17.____
    D. summary E. tomato

131

18.	A. occur	B. villain	C. disastrous	18.____
	D. entirely	E. calculater		
19.	A. hurrying	B. immense	C. aggressive	19.____
	D. victim	E. exclusivly		
20.	A. businesslike	B. miracle	C. equipment	20.____
	D. explanatory	E. division		

KEY (CORRECT ANSWERS)

CORRECT SPELLING

1. E, lying
2. A, glossary
3. E, impressionable
4. B, hereditary
5. C, apparently
6. E, unanimous
7. A, suspicion
8. D, usually
9. A, ridiculous
10. D, unison

CORRECT SPELLING

11. B, technique
12. C, shining
13. D, infancy
14. C, observant
15. B, transferred
16. D, persistent
17. B, jewelry
18. E, calculator
19. E, exclusively
20. D, explanatory

TEST 4

DIRECTIONS: In each of the following groups of words, only one of the words is misspelled. In each group, select the misspelled word and then write the letter of your choice in the answer space at the right.

1. A. rapture B. fictitious C. inocence 1.____
   D. humorous E. cyclical

2. A. abnormality B. fidelity C. hybrid 2.____
   D. harpoon E. antaganist

3. A. actually B. interupt C. inspiration 3.____
   D. equipped E. squirrel

4. A. hypothisis B. popularity C. hypnosis 4.____
   D. acceptable E. convertible

5. A. inconveniance B. humidity C. ninety 5.____
   D. radiant E. campaign

6. A. caucus B. secede C. gallent 6.____
   D. erroneous E. crisis

7. A. interaction B. coalition C. philosophy 7.____
   D. guarantee E. treachary

8. A. prairie B. propeller C. strategy 8.____
   D. divisible E. secretery

9. A. merchant B. obsticle C. parcel 9.____
   D. altitude E. ignorant

10. A. choral B. acommodate C. capacity 10.____
    D. neighborly E. deodorant

11. A. arrangement B. gradually C. portable 11.____
    D. aristocrat E. junction

12. A. umbrella B. grandeur C. familar 12.____
    D. infinite E. calorie

13. A. purgatory B. inprisonment C. hopeless 13.____
    D. division E. awkward

14. A. fascinate B. disimilar C. luscious 14.____
    D. immaculate E. persuasive

15. A. traffic B. senseless C. rhythm 15.____
    D. acclaim E. grammar

16. A. stagnation B. ambivalence C. twelfth 16.____
    D. territory E. adherance

17. A. desireable B. physics C. predominant 17.____
    D. malaria E. corrupt

133

18. A. nuisance   B. hysteria   C. equivalent   18.___
    D. development E. ratify

19. A. faulty   B. seize   C. suspence   19.___
    D. tomorrow   E. traction

20. A. reliable   B. luxurious   C. preoccupied   20.___
    D. carrying   E. divisable

KEY (CORRECT ANSWERS)

CORRECT SPELLING

1. C, innocence
2. E, antagonist
3. B, interrupt
4. A, hypothesis
5. A, inconvenience
6. C, gallant
7. E, treachery
8. E, secretary
9. B, obstacle
10. B, accommodate

CORRECT SPELLING

11. D, aristocrat
12. C, familiar
13. B, imprisonment
14. B, dissimilar
15. D, acclaim
16. E, adherence
17. A, desirable
18. C, equivalent
19. C, suspense
20. E, divisible

TEST 5

DIRECTIONS: In each of the following groups of words, only one of the words is misspelled. In each group, select the misspelled word and then write the letter of your choice in the answer space at the right.

1. A. candidate   B. merchandise   C. soloes   1._____
   D. source   E. siphon

2. A. scent   B. sovereign   C. banana   2._____
   D. gardner   E. career

3. A. theoretical B. bagage   C. consequence   3._____
   D. bargain   E. encouraging

4. A. simultaneous B. leisure   C. twilight   4._____
   D. cloride   E. muffle

5. A. excessive   B. pennant   C. misfit   5._____
   D. vineger   E. kerosene

6. A. strength   B. medley   C. cannibal   6._____
   D. reciept   E. decency

7. A. accidentally B. shield   C. advising   7._____
   D. treasury   E. disconfort

8. A. vengeful   B. miniature   C. alliance   8._____
   D. comprehensable E. prohibited

9. A. psychiatrist B. grievance   C. barbecue   9._____
   D. formerly   E. controled

10. A. journel   B. shadowy   C. tomorrow   10._____
    D. convertible E. macaroni

11. A. despair   B. receiver   C. instance   11._____
    D. langauge   E. convertible

12. A. brevity   B. height   C. apolegy   12._____
    D. shield   E. engagement

13. A. acceptence B. arbitrary   C. hypnotism   13._____
    D. physician E. quarrel

14. A. zoology   B. armory   C. cemetery   14._____
    D. frivolous E. honorery

15. A. triple   B. tough   C. trifel   15._____
    D. tongue   E. terrible

16. A. luscious   B. adaquate   C. temporary   16._____
    D. ghostly   E. umbrella

17. A. genuine   B. hygeine   C. omission   17._____
    D. sincerely E. bracelet

135

18.	A. symptom	B. specialty	C. available	18.____
	D. skeleton	E. flammible		
19.	A. spaghetti	B. locale	C. practice	19.____
	D. worthyness	E. parcel		
20.	A. testamonial	B. corruption	C. aggravate	20.____
	D. apathetic	E. tissue		

KEY (CORRECT ANSWERS)

	CORRECT SPELLING		CORRECT SPELLING
1.	C, solos	11.	D, language
2.	D, gardener	12.	C, apology
3.	B, baggage	13.	A, acceptance
4.	D, chloride	14.	E, honorary
5.	D, vinegar	15.	C, trifle
6.	D, receipt	16.	B, adequate
7.	E, discomfort	17.	B, hygiene
8.	D, comprehensible	18.	E, flammable
9.	E, controlled	19.	D, worthiness
10.	A, journal	20.	A, testimonial

www.ingramcontent.com/pod-product-compliance
Lightning Source LLC
Chambersburg PA
CBHW082124230426
43671CB00015B/2796